ALPHABET ARTS

Learning Letters Through Sensory Experiences

by Kathy Faggella
and
Janet Horowitz

Art by Kathy Faggella

First Teacher Press
First Teacher, Inc./Bridgeport, CT

DEDICATION

This book is dedicated to Jim, Katie, Ari, Rachel, and Leah
With fond memories of all the hours we spent together learning the letters of the alphabet.

A special thanks to our refrigerators which withstood many years of having plastic magnet letters scraped across them.

Copyright © 1987, Kathy Faggella, Janet Horowitz

All rights reserved; except for the inclusion of brief quotations in a review or for classroom use, no part of this book may be reproduced in any form without written permission form the publisher.

ISBN 09615005-7-3

Library of Congress Catalog Number 87-083160

Design by Karen Baumann

Cover design by Alice Cooke: Photograph by Margo Retz
Edited by Lisa Lyons Durkin

Assistant Editor: Kathleen Hyson

Layout and Typesetting: Michael Pearl

Manufactured in the United States of America

Published by First Teacher Press, First Teacher, Inc.
P.O. Box 29, 60 Main Street, Bridgeport, CT 06602

Distributed by: Gryphon House
        P.O. Box 275
        Mt. Ranier, MD 20712

Table of Contents

Introduction   7
    Children and Learning   8
    Children and Letters   11
    How to Use this Book   12
    Create an Alphabet Corner   13

A
The Old Woman with 26 Children (*story*)   15
Alphabet Apron   16
Follow-up Activities   17

B
Bendable Barney (*poem*)   19
Bendable Beads   20
Follow-up Activities   21

C
Alphabet Cakes (*poem*)   23
Cookie Cutter   24
Follow-up Activities   25

D
Chocolate Mazes (*game*)   27
Dessert Letters   28
Follow-up Activities   29

E
The Surprise Garden (*story*)   31
From the Earth Letters   32
Follow-up Activities   33

F
Paints (*poem*)   35
Foot and Finger Paints   36
Follow-up Activities   37

G
Giant Blocks (*story*)   39
Giant Blocks   40
Follow-up Activities   41

H
Changes, Changes (*poem*)   43
Hard/Soft Letters   44
Follow-up Activities   45

I
I Am (*mini-play*)   47
"I" Puppets   48
Follow-up Activities   49

J
The Jiggle Dance (*dance*)   51
Jiggling Letters   52
Follow-up Activities   53

K
K (*concrete poem*)   55
Kitchen Sculpture   56
Follow-up Activities   57

L
The Sweetest Lullaby in the World (*story*)   59
Lullaby Dream Pillow   60
Follow-up Activities   61

M
M Marvin's Marvelous Magical M (*story*)   63
Marvelous Munchible Letters   64
Follow-up Activities   65

N
N Photo Album (*activity*)   67
Neighborhood Mural   68
Follow-up Activities   69

O
O The Clever Kingdom (*story*)   71
Overstuffed Letters   72
Follow-up Activities   73

P
P Prince Peter Finds his Princess (*story*)   75
Pasta Letters   76
Follow-up Activities   77

Q
Q Appliqued Quilt (*game*)   79
Quilt Letter   80
Follow-up Activities   81

R
R "You and I Together" (*song*)   83
Rubber Stamps   84
Follow-up Activities   85

S
S Sand (*poem*)   87
Sand Letters   88
Follow-up Activities   89

T Follow the Alphabet (*game*) 91
Letters in Trays 92
Follow-up Activities 93

U U Alphabert (*story*) 95
Uniform Letters 96
Follow-up Activities 97

V V What If... (*poem*) 99
Very Soft Letters Bowling 100
Follow-up Activities 101

W W Watch Out for Winston (*story*) 103
Wooly Stabiles 104
Follow-up Activities 105

X X Pen and Ink Games (*game*) 107
X-tra Special Inks 108
Follow-up Activities 109

Y Y The Sampler (*story*) 111
Yarn Letters 112
Follow-up Activities 113

Z Z A Zoo Alphabet (*poem*) 115
Zoo Box 116
Follow-up Activities 117

Have an Alphabet Party 118
Block Letters 122

WE BELIEVE THAT

- children learn through all of their senses (taste, touch, sight, smell, and sound).

- teachers should familiarize themselves with each child's best learning modality (visual, auditory, or kinesthetic) in order to teach most effectively.

- teachers should teach to all the senses using a variety of media and manipulative materials.

- children learn best through a variety of first-hand experiences.

- children learn through the movements of their bodies; through the muscles of their hands, feet, heads, and whole body.

- children need to know the alphabet in order to eventually build words and sentences that communicate and convey their ideas, feelings, and thoughts.

- children need to interact and play with letters in many different forms (that appeal to all the senses) in order to visually and auditorily discriminate their appearance and sounds.

- children should have the opportunity to use various artistic media to provide them with many sensory learning experiences, particularly in learning letters.

- children can "learn to like to learn" and be successful students with our encouragement, positive energy, and excitement for learning.

- children who are self-confident and feel good about themselves increase their enjoyment and ability to learn.

Children and Learning

The young child is as an artist's canvas, all primed and awaiting the first dabs of color that will transform it into a one-of-a-kind creation. Each new experience and each new sensation color and add form and substance to this piece of art.

Just as brush and paints are the tools and materials of the artist, the senses, through everyday encounters and experiences, are the tools with which the young child works. They transmit and interpret reality for the child and gradually shape and mold him into a unique masterpiece.

The shape and size of the canvas often suggests what the final painting will turn out to be. The same is true of the child. He brings to the world his own characteristics and interprets life within the restrictions and dimensions he has available. It is so fortunate that both the canvas and the child have so very many possibilities!

It is to these possibilities that we teach. It is the whole palette of experience that we can offer. And, we have a most willing student in the child with his natural curiosity and boundless energy to pursue answers to his questions.

There are three important beliefs that we hold about learning for the young child.

• Their learning occurs through their senses and is internalized in their whole bodies.

• Learning must be experiential and first-hand.

• There is or should be an integration in teaching so all knowledge has a connectedness, a wholeness rather than fragmentation.

Learning Through the Senses

As adults, so many of our vivid memories of childhood are rediscovered through the sights, sounds, feel, tastes, and even smells of today that are reminiscent of those earlier times. We learned through our senses and they create powerful memories. Newborn infants are totally dependent on their senses to tell them about the world. The young child continually uses all of his senses to gain knowledge of the world, himself, and to develop mobility and language.

Children learn through all their senses, selecting the one most appropriate for each task or situation. Most children, as well as adults, do tend to have a dominant or stronger sense, however. This is the sense—be it auditory, visual, or kinesthetic—through which they learn best. The other senses reinforce the learning that occurs through the dominant sense. Therefore, in teaching children, we need to teach to all the senses. That way, we know we are teaching to each child's dominant sense and giving support and reinforcement of that same knowledge through the less dominant senses.

Sensory learning is more than isolated stimuli; it is whole body learning. Children learn knowledge and information with their whole bodies. It becomes internalized from the skin right down

to the bones, muscles, and joints. That is why, when learning new information such as letters, we encourage children to trace or 'walk' a letter, or to bend their bodies to be that letter. Children must move to learn. Clapping and tapping the rhythms to songs or poems enhance learning patterns. Learning should be an integration of the visual, auditory, and kinesthetic modes.

Experiential Learning

Because sensory learning is so very important to the young child, we can see that children learn experientially. They must experience and do things first-hand. It is not enough to just tell them about a bird's nest. They must see one, preferably in its original location, then feel the twigs, string, and soil around it. They must touch its delicate, yet sturdy, walls. They need to listen to its hardness as it is set upon a table. In this way, all their senses have been fed.

Experiential learning also means that a child must DO something, perhaps over and over, until that knowledge is genuinely his. An old Chinese proverb says,

> I hear and I forget,
> I see and I remember,
> I do and I understand.

Children must interact with an object or with a piece of knowledge to truly know it. Watch a young child on his first encounter with play dough. For days, he will just pull, smash, and poke at it. These activities are necessary in order for him to understand this material called "play dough." It is only when his need to manipulate the play dough is satisfied that he can begin to use it to to make abstract representations of real objects. He understands the material and what it can do and is able to use it for what he wants.

Children should be given the opportunity to experience information in many ways. In this way, learning is exciting and more apt to be 'caught' by the child. In this book, learning the alphabet by craft work, observations, listening to stories and poems, playing games, and participating in movement activities gives children a broad experiential base. It innundates their senses and provides opportunities to use and play with the knowledge in unique ways until it is theirs for life. Children must have this broad experiential background to realize the relationship of the sounds that they hear and make to the letters that symbolize those sounds.

The Wholeness and Integration of Learning

For the young child, every new day brings new information about the world. As a very young child, that information comes in bits and pieces and eventually the child synthesizes it into a whole picture that suggests the world.

We make these connections as we teach the young child. We teach with thematic units and integrate all the methods, materials, and media we have available. For each theme, we sing songs, do artwork, role play, examine and experiment scientifically, as well as read and listen to the literature on the subject. There is a wholeness in presenting a theme in this manner.

Learning letters is no exception to this type of learning. Even if we choose to teach one letter a week, as so many of us are accustomed to doing, we can surround each letter with activities that draw from the creative arts, music, and literature. We can reinforce the letter with games and creative movement. This type of 'total immersion' will result in making the children conscious of letters around them. They will be able to discern and name each letter but, also, they will see that letters make up words and that the written word is really symbols for their spoken word.

Communication—both written and spoken—is, for us human beings, as basic a necessity as is food, sleep, the craving for beauty, and love.

Children and Letters

To the young child, letters are:

- toys to touch
- symbols that are part of their everyday environment
- playing pieces for games
- smile and praise-getters
- keys to unlock the mystery of words

Letters are toys to touch.

Letters are the wooden blocks and plastic magnets on the refrigerator that are fun to play with, suck on, and throw.

Young children are exposed to letters in all forms at very early ages. Although they treat them as no more than toys, letters are still there for them to touch, hold, and become familiar with.

Letters are symbols that are part of children's everyday environment.

Letters are the colorful billboards along the roadside, the decorations on cereal boxes, and the content of notes written by Mom and Dad. They surround the pictures in books and magazines and are seen flashing on T.V.

At first only parts of pictures, letters eventually become distinctive symbols that have names and can be discerned in various sizes and colors, while still maintaining their basic shape.

Letters are playing pieces for games.

Letters are objects used to play "Guess Its Name," "Make Its Sound," and "Match It to Another One that Looks the Same."

Young children use letters as playing pieces in games with adults. These games appear to be simple, fun activities that take place as the child is taking a bath or playing with his toys. Yet, there is sophisticated learning going on since the games are really stressing visual and auditory discrimination with the adult providing positive reinforcement.

Letters are smile and praise-getters.

Letter names are great to know and recite for getting attention from adults.

Young children learn very quickly that their ability to recite letter names and do matching games win excited reactions from adults. The instant response and approval sparks in children the desire to learn more in order to please and thereby receive more attention.

Letters are keys that unlock the mystery of words.

Letters eventually begin to be seen by the child as parts of a whole—like cars on a train that can exist separately, but have pulling power when connected into words.

Young children put letters together to make their names as one of the first words they learn to recognize and write. With this single activity, they have learned that letters combined together make one, special word that names one special object—namely themselves! As the mystery of words further unfolds, children learn that they can express themselves with these letters when they are put together.

How to Use This Book

Alphabet Arts is a guide that shows you how to enrich and enhance the teaching of the letters of the alphabet to young children. We suggest specific activities and projects that provide children with fun ways of learning letters with many different kinds of concrete materials. We show how teaching the alphabet in a multi-sensory fashion can be used as an integrated part of the curriculum, how it can stimulate the imagination, and encourage creative thinking.

The letters and activities are interchangeable, giving you hundreds of ideas to enhance learning.

Each chapter is organized with an introductory story, poem, or game; a related craft; and follow-up enrichment activities. It is best to read the story, poem, or play the game first and then do the craft and other follow-up activities. This link between the story, poem, or game to a letter and craft gives more meaning and substance to the teaching of that letter. Some of the introductory pages may be reproduced and given to the children to use. The followups provide other activities using the letters that have just been crafted or the craft material in an extended way.

There are 26 chapters for the 26 letters of the alphabet. However, the crafts are paired with letters at random so that any craft project can be used for any letter that you are teaching. When your class is studying a particular letter , use this book as a resource for many different ways to present and teach that letter. Choose the ones that are most appropriate for the age and ability of your children. If you are planning to teach only one letter per week, use a variety of techniques, textures, and sizes. It's lovely to bombard the room with the letter of the week in many different media. Also, try to choose some of the activities that would fit into an existing class theme. For example, if you are studying transportation, do license plate rubbings, set up the sign-making shop for words on vehicles, and so on. In this way, learning the letters is integrated into all aspects of the children's learning.

Bring many of a child's senses into each craft experience.

As children are making their crafted alphabet letter, have them hear the letter pronounced many times, have them feel how the letter is formed, with its curves and/or straight lines, and maybe discuss the texture of the material. This will bring other senses into this learning experience.

Each craft page is a mini-poster that can be hung up as the letter is being crafted. You might also wish to send a copy to parents for followup at home.

We've chosen to use only capital letters as examples throughout the book. For your convenience, there is a block letter alphabet at the back of the book. They can be enlarged at your local photostat store. However, we believe that young children should be taught both upper and lower case letters from the beginning since they will be expected to know them when they reach the primary grades. Thus, the alphabet crafts and activities in this book may be used to teach letters in any form.

Create an Alphabet Corner

Things to Put in the Alphabet Corner

Somewhere in your classroom or school, find a spot that can be made into an Alphabet Corner. This will be a place to spotlight individual letters, to display beautiful letter crafts, and to provide a storage center—an area where children can interact with letters of all sorts.

There are some basic alphabet-related objects you might like to put into this corner:

• Alphabet books—some on shelves and some on display.

• Alphabet games—both commercial ones and ones you've made from this book. Put each game into a sturdy box, label the end, and stack onto shelves for children to take out and use as they desire.

• Alphabets and individual letters that you've purchased. Some of the more beautiful ones can be hung and displayed. Others might be set out each day for children to use—such as stamp sets or pasta.

• Alphabet crafts. As you make a craft from this book, place a sample of the finished product in the Alphabet Corner. Many children will often copy the process again on their own. Children also love to play with things that have become familiar to them.

• A display shelf and/or bulletin board for the "Letter of the Week." Save this spot to announce the letter to children and parents and to display a particular craft children will do.

• A box to collect small objects that can be used in letter-object match games and activities. This is where you put the old zipper and tooth X-ray you've begged from your dentist.

• Soft cushions and/or a quilt (made from directions on page 80) for children to sit on and cuddle up to for reading, game playing, and "just relaxing."

Make this area a vibrant part of your classroom.

Make the Alphabet Corner a vibrant part of your classroom. Introduce new letters there. Demonstrate how to use any new game or activity you might store there. Bring children in to read an ABC book once a week.

Carefully serve an alphabet snack in the area. Let children choose the Alphabet Corner for individual and free play. And most of all, keep it fresh and interesting by changing displays often and continually adding new things. Children will share your enthusiasm and excitement!

Alphabet Apron

THE OLD WOMAN WITH 26 CHILDREN

Once, there was an old woman who lived in a shoe. She had 26 children and didn't know what to do. Her children were named from A to Z. There was Annie, Bob, Carol, Danny, Ed, Frank, George, Hildie, Ida, and Jim. There was Kate, Leah, Milly, Ned, Olga, Pete, Quinn, Randy, Sam, and Tim. There was also Ulysses, Vivien, Walter, Xanadu, Yvonne, and Zebulon. So you can imagine the confusion everyday when the old woman called each in from play to eat their supper of bread and broth.

At first, she called each by name, but, often she would forget one or two and it just took so long that by the time she had called Zebulon, Annie had eaten her supper! So she finally decided to just call out the letters of the alphabet.

"Oh, A, B,C,D, E, F, G," all the way to Z she called and each came home to supper. But every once in a while, one of her children didn't come home , and it wasn't until bedtime that she missed him or her. So the old woman had to think of a way to make sure she knew all her children were at home.

Being such a clever woman, she made a large apron with 26 pockets. On each pocket was one letter of the alphabet from A to Z. She wore the apron as she called her children in for supper. Each child had to bring an object that started with the initial of his or her name and place it into the proper apron pocket. So Annie brought an apricot, Bob brought a box, Carol some coal, and right on down the line to Zebulon who placed a zipper into the apron pocket.

All went very well each evening as the old woman checked her apron and made sure each pocket was filled with one object from each child.

All went well . . . except for one evening. She looked at her apron and found the ball from Bob, the coal from Carol, a dollar from Danny, but--there was no acorn from Annie! Her A pocket was empty! There was nothing in it. Annie was missing!

But wait! You can help Annie get back home. All you have to do is find something that begins with the letter A right where you are. Then, call out Annie's name and she will surely get home safe and sound!

ALPHABET APRON

YOU'LL NEED:

a whole sheet of newspaper

1¼ yds plain fabric (muslin, denim, canvas)

sewing machine

pins

ruler

pencil

permanent marker

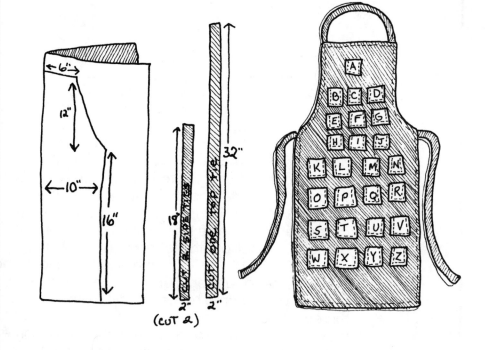

6"

12"

10"

16"

32"

18"

CUT 2 SIDE TIES

CUT ONE TOP TIE

2"

2"

(CUT 2)

A B C D E F G H I J K L M N O P Q R S T U V W X Y Z

WHAT TO DO:

1. Adult makes a paper pattern for the apron by folding a whole sheet of newspaper in half — bottom to top.

2. Turn paper so fold is on left side and measure and mark as shown above. Draw pattern and cut out.

3. Place pattern on fabric. Trace around it and cut out. Fold all edges back ½" and sew down.

4. Cut three fabric strips as directed above. Fold each strip in half and sew ¼" in from raw edges—the whole length.

5. Sew side ties to apron, and sew each end of top tie to a corner of apron top. Cut 26, 4" square pockets. Fold all edges back ¼" and sew.

6. Pin pockets on as illustrated. Sew down long three sides ¼" from edges. Use marker to write one alphabet letter on each pocket.

Follow-up Activities

Fill My Pockets!

Ask children to put any "little" objects that they find around the room that starts with the letter that you are studying into that pocket of the Alphabet Apron. At the end of the day, share what is in the pocket. (You might want to have one or two of your own surprises in the pocket.)

Find The Pin

Fasten a large safety pin, costume jewelry pin, or clothespin to one of the pockets. Ask children to tell you on which letter it is fastened. Change the pin to different pockets on other days.

"I Know the Alphabet" T-shirt

Instruct each parent to send in a solid white T-shirt for their child to use during the year. Place a heavy piece of cardboard between the front and back of the T-shirt. On the front of each child's T-shirt, write (with permanent markers) "I know the alphabet." After the child has mastered a letter, have him write that letter on his shirt with a permanent marker. When the whole alphabet is learned, the child can sign his name on the shirt and wear it home.

Letter Hat

With a pin, attach a paper or felt letter to the front of a baseballl-style cap. Everyone should be able to see the letter except the person wearing the hat. Have other children act out a word that starts with that letter or, in some way, use their bodies, arms, or fingers to make the letter. When the child wearing the hat guesses correctly, he puts the hat with another mystery letter onto another child.
• Variation The child, wearing the letter hat, knows what the letter is and has to act out something that starts with that letter for the other children to guess. The one who guesses gets to wear the hat next.

Alphabet Jump

Draw a large letter on a pillowcase or brown paper bag. Give one to each child and let him color it in. Cut out holes for the head and arms to slip through. Have children line up in their letter shirts and sing the "Alphabet Song." When a child hears his letter, he has to jump in front. If you have less than 26 children, draw a letter on the back of the pillowcase or bag, also. When that letter is sung, the child turns around and jumps one step backwards! You can also use these letter costumes to spell out lots of different messages, such as "Happy New Year," "Welcome," and "Good-Bye."

Letter Labels

Attach little felt letters with safety pins to children's clothes that start with that letter. For example, put an S on a shoe and a shirt, a B on a belt, a P on pants, and so on.

Bendable Beads

BENDABLE BARNEY

Bendable Barney
        broke a bone
    while trying to sit
        on his telephone.

Bendable Barney
        hurt his head
    while trying to dive
        into a waterbed.

Bendable Barney
        scraped his knee
    while trying to jump
        into a cup of tea.

Bendable Barney
        sprained his back
    while trying to sleep
        in an old backpack.

Bendable Barney
        bruised his hand
    while trying to sail
        a boat on land.

Bendable Barney
    thought he was so great,
        but, unfortunately,
        learned a little too late,
That 'though his body could curve and bend
    pain was all he had
        in the end.
So don't be like Barney
        and use your skills
            to do such silly things--

BENDABLE BEAD LETTERS

YOU'LL NEED:

one piece green floral wire (or 18 gauge coiled wire)

wooden beads

scrap blocks of wood

stapler   STAPLE GUN

needlenose pliers

WHAT TO DO:

1. Adult bends wire one half inch up at one end and staples that end to center of a scrap piece of wood.

2. Children string beads on wire to within $\frac{1}{2}$" of end. Adult uses pliers to bend wire end into a loop to hold beads in place.

3. Children bend this bead sculpture into various letters.

Follow-up Activities

Bendable Beads

Have children string other materials onto wire in place of beads--marshmallows, macaroni, cereals.

Alphabet Chute

Mark letters on each of 10 beads. Set up a chute with a long, empty giftwrap tube. Have one child sit on one end of the tube, choose one letter bead and place it into the tube. Let the bead roll down to the other end where another child (or children) name it and keep it. Children switch places after all beads are used.

Alphabet Slide

Construct this slide in the same manner as Bendable Bead Letters, except using heavier and longer wire, such as coiled 18 or 20 gauge wire available in hardware stores. Attach one end to large wood scrap (with a staple gun) and bend and curve so that it extends upward. Fold top end of wire over slightly so it is not sharp. Let children drop a bead with a letter on it down the wire and watch it twist and turn on the way down.
- *Variation 1* Put two wires of the same length on one piece of wood. Start two beads at once and see which drops the fastest.
- *Variation 2* Put beads on the wire in ABC order.

Initial Beads

Have children make their own letter beads out of clay or play dough (See page 65.) Have them carve or paint a letter onto each bead to make their names. String each bead onto yarn to wear as a necklace.

Name Bracelet

Using storebought letter beads, have children string the letters of their names onto stretchy elastic thread. Knot well and wear.

Letter Sculptures

Make large bendable letters by stringing orange juice cans (with lids removed), paper towel tubes, oatmeal boxes, or toilet tissue tubes onto large wire.

Cookie Cutter

ALPHABET   CAKES

Apple
Banana
Chocolate
　　　and
Dates
　　　Ah! Those are my favorite cakes.
Egg Nog
Fruit
Green Grape
　　　and
Hot
　　　Wow! I like them all a lot!
Ice Cream
Jelly
Kumquat
　　　and
Lime
　　　Oh! Those flavors are sublime!
Marble
Nut
Orange
　　　and
Pound
　　　Gee! Those are some of the best around!
Quince
Raspberry
Strawberry
　　　and
Tart
　　　Gosh, those all are dear to my heart!
Upside
　　　Down
Vanilla
　　　and
Walnut
　　　Really! I can think of no better, but
　　　with
Xtra Frosting
Yellow
　　　and
Zucchini
　　　My taste for cakes makes sure I'll not be teeny!

COOKIE CUTTER

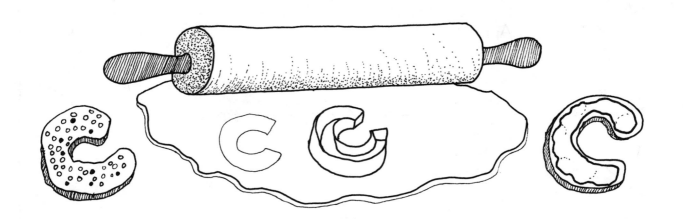

YOU'LL NEED:

aluminum flashing

tin snips

emery paper

work gloves

needlenose pliers

WHAT TO DO:

1. Adult uses tin snips to cut an 18" long by 1" wide piece of aluminum flashing. (Cut a longer length if letter has many sides)

2. Wearing work gloves and using needlenose pliers, adult bends aluminum flashing strip into a letter shape

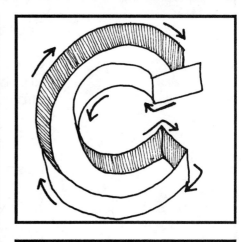

3. With pliers, adult folds back ¼" of aluminum strip at both ends of letter (in preparation to join ends)

★ Use emery paper to smooth edges.

4. Slip one end under the other to attach.

Follow-up Activities

Aluminum Cutter Uses

Use the cutters to cut letters out of :
- Cookie dough (See following recipe.)
- Bread slices
- Bread/play dough (See page 64.)

Sugar Cookie Recipe

You'll Need:
- 3 1/2 cups flour
- 2 1/2 teaspoons baking powder
- 2 eggs
- 1 teaspoon vanilla
- 1 teaspoon salt
- 1 1/2 cup sugar
- 1 tablespoon milk
- 2/3 cup shortening

What to Do:

1. Help children mix shortening, sugar, eggs, and vanilla until fluffy.

2. Have children add flour mixed with baking powder, and salt. Add milk.

3.Have children mix well. Form into a ball of dough and refrigerate for one hour.

4. Roll to 1/4 inch thick. Have children cut with aluminum cutters.

5. Place on greased cookie sheets and bake at 400 degrees F for nine minutes.

Giant Cookie Puzzle

Cut a large letter from cookie dough. Place on cookie sheet and score it almost all the way through with a knife into large puzzle pieces. Bake until browned . Cool and gently break into puzzle pieces. Have children put the letter together, identify it, and then, eat it.

Gingerbread Alphabet Horn Books

In Colonial days at holiday time, children received gingerbread cookies shaped like horn books, wrapped in gold or silver paper. If the child could say all the alphabet letters that had been scratched into the dough, he could eat it.

Carry on this old tradition by having children write all their own letters--or at least all the ones they can.

Here is the recipe for Gingerbread Horn Books.

You'll Need:
- 1 cup brown sugar
- 1 1/2 cups molasses
- 1/3 cup shortening
- 2/3 cup water
- 6-7 cups flour

- 1/2 teaspoon cinnamon
- 1/2 teaspoon nutmeg
- 1/2 teaspoon ginger
- 1 teaspoon salt
- 2 teaspoons baking soda

What to Do:

1. Help children combine the first four ingredients.
2. Have them mix together the next six ingredients.
3. Add the dry ingredients to sugar-molasses mixture and water.
4. Have children mix well. Roll or pat dough on surface. Adult uses a knife to cut out hornbook shapes (a square with a handle on bottom). Child uses toothpick to scratch in letters.
5. Bake on greased cookie sheet at 350 degrees F for 15 minutes. Cool and wrap in foil.

Mashed Potato Letters

Make a bowl of instant mashed potatoes and let children make letter shapes out of the potatoes, spooning them directly on a baking sheet. Coat each letter with a beaten egg and brown it in the oven at 350 degrees F for 15-20 minutes.

Rainbow Sandwich Letters

Help children construct a triple decker sandwich with bread, one layer of one color jelly, bread, layer of cream cheese, bread, layer of another color jelly, and bread. Have them hold cookie cutter over top piece of bread and push all the way down through the sandwich.

Book to Read

Read A Apple Pie: An Old Fashion Alphabet Book by Kate Greenaway with children.

Dessert Letters

Directions:
   Start at the star and trace a path inside the chocolate lines going across the page to each chocolate treat.
   Variation: Make your own chocolate maze by squeezing melted chocolate onto waxed paper in a maze shape.

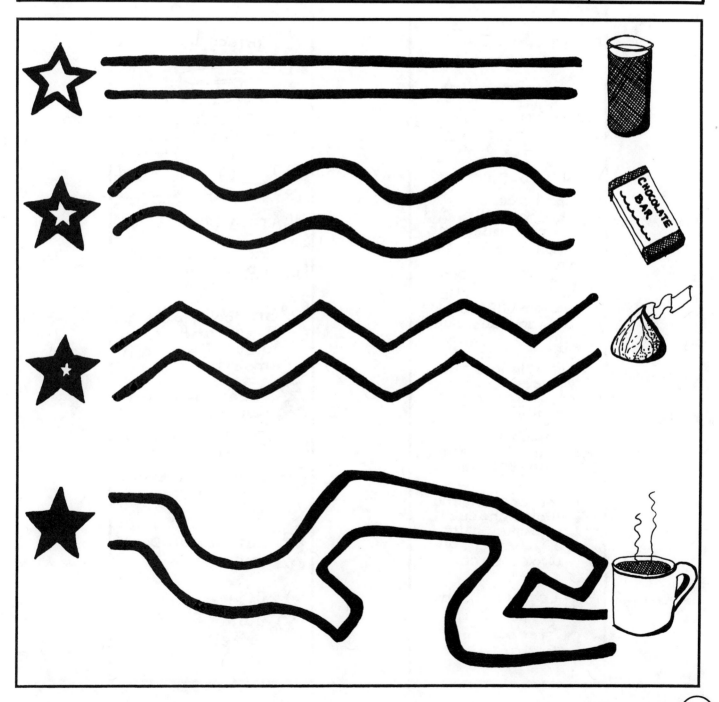

DESSERT LETTERS

Chocolate

YOU'LL NEED:

 6 oz. semisweet chocolate bits

 1 tblsp. melted vegetable shortening

heat proof jar

 saucepan

clean squeeze bottle

 MUSTARD

WAXED PAPER

WHAT TO DO:

1. Child places chocolate bits and shortening in jar. Adult places jar in saucepan with simmering water until chocolate melts. (If you have a microwave oven, put the bits and shortening directly into the squeeze bottle and microwave on HI for 2 min.)

2. Spoon melted chocolate into squeeze bottle.

3. Squeeze slightly cooled chocolate into the shape of a letter on waxed paper.

4. Let cool ½ hour or place in freezer for 5 minutes.

FROSTING

YOU'LL NEED:

 3 egg whites

1 pound confectionary sugar

1 tsp. lemon juice

rotary beater

bowl

WAXED PAPER

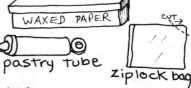 pastry tube

ziplock bag   cut

WHAT TO DO:

1. Place egg whites in bowl and beat until foamy.

2. Gradually add sugar and lemon juice. Beat until smooth.

3. Place frosting in pastry tube or ziplocking bag. (Clip one corner off)

4. Squeeze frosting letters onto waxed paper.

5. Let dry on paper overnight.

6. Peel paper away from letter.

Follow-up Activities

Chocolate Chip Letters

- Place chocolate chips in the form of a letter on a cookie sheet and bake.
- Place chocolate chips in a dot-to-dot fashion and connect with squeezed melted chocolate.

Squeeze Letters

- Have children make squeeze letters out of whipped cream, shaving cream, or cheese in a can .
- Help them squeeze cream cheese, diluted with milk, onto fruit slices or crackers and decorate with olives or cherries.

  Place anything to be squeezed into a zip-locking bag. Squeeze air out and seal tightly. Cut corner off one side of bag bottom and squeeze.

Alphabet Ornaments

Place Royal Frosting (recipe on preceding page) into a zip-locking bag. Cut corner and have children squeeze a letter shape onto waxed paper. Let dry overnight. Help children tie bright yarn or ribbon on the letter and hang on a holiday evergreen or an anyday branch to make an alphabet tree.

Molded Chocolate Letters

Melt chocolate chips (or melting caps) and pour or squeeze into commercial candy molds. Tap mold on counter twice. Freeze for five minutes and pop out of mold.

Bread Letters

Have children paint letters onto bread with milk and food coloring. (Use several tablespoons of milk with a few drops of food coloring.) Then, toast.

Glue Frosting

Using Royal Frosting as a glue, Help children to make letters out of circle and stick storebought pretzels. Letters must be made on wax paper so that, after they dry, they can be peeled off. Use as decorations for trees or room.

From the Earth Letters

THE SURPRISE GARDEN

One fine morning, Oliver Greenthumb was walking down the lane and spied a small package lying on the road a few feet ahead of him. He looked around and, seeing no one in sight, he bent down and picked it up. Oliver shook the package and it made a small rattling sound. It appeared to be a packet of seeds. On the outside of the package was written "Plant Us!"

"*I wonder what kind of seeds these are,*" he thought. He slipped them into his vest pocket, straightened his cap, and walked home.

When he got home, Oliver opened the seed packet. To his surprise, instead of the usual seeds, he found tiny seeds in the shape of letters! He immediately began to sort the seeds into small into small piles. There were E's, T's, C's, B's, L's, P's, and S's.

"*What a strange thing this is,*" said Oliver Greenthumb right out loud. "*I'm going to plant these seeds and see what grows.*"

So Oliver Greenthumb planted each type of letter seed in one row of the garden. Sure enough, at harvest time, Oliver had neat rows of vegetables and each row had vegetables that started with the same letter.

Can you put the vegetables in Oliver's garden? Make sure you put them in the proper rows.

from the earth letters

YOU'LL NEED:

shallow container

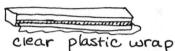
clear plastic wrap

potting soil

parsley, alfalfa, or other herb or sprouting seeds

plant mister

WHAT TO DO:

1. Child lines container with plastic wrap. Child adds soil to depth of $1\frac{1}{2}"-2"$.

2. Child presses one finger very lightly into soil to make a large letter impression.

3. Child sprinkles the seeds sparsely into the letter impression in the soil.

4. Child sprinkles the seeds with about $\frac{1}{16}"$ thick cover of fine soil.

5. Child moistens whole tray well with plant mister. Adult covers the pan with plastic wrap.

6. Set pan out of direct sunlight until seeds begin to sprout. Then remove cover and place in direct sunlight.

Follow-up Activities

Grocery Store

Introduce this activity by bringing in or taking a class trip to the supermarket to buy the vegetables that begin with the letters mentioned in the story. With the vegetables in front of children, read the story and have them brainstorm which ones they think start with the letter E, S, P , and so on. Have them sort these into letter piles. On a large sheet of paper, write the name (and a quick sketch) of each vegetable mentioned. Next, you are ready to have children do the reproduced activity from page 31. You may want to take another trip to a grocery store and have the children identify the vegetables again.

Alphabet Seed or Bean Toss

Mark each cavity of an egg carton with a different letter. Have children toss the beans into the egg carton and identify the letter that it lands in.

Message Seed Pots

Plant flower seeds in dirt-filled styrofoam cups that have a few pencil points punched in the bottom for drainage. Using permanent markers, write one letter on each cup to spell out a message such as "Happy Spring." Put the message cups on a sunny windowsill as a lovely decoration.

Mosaic Seed Letter

Gather pebbles, twigs, and large seeds--pumpkin, squash, sunflower, dried beans. Draw a block letter on a piece of heavy paper or posterboard. Have children spread a small area with glue and attach one type of seed. Have them continue spreading glue in small areas and filling in the letter with the rest of the natural materials available.

Foot and Finger Paints

PAINTINGS

(This little chant can be recited as children make fingerpainted letters or use the paint to draw letters on their bodies.)

Fingers, fingers
Thumb
and hand
Make my paintings

best in the land!

Toe, toe
Sole
and heel
Make my paintings

great to feel!

Fist, fist
Elbow
and wrist
Make my paintings

with a twist!

Arm, arm
Foot
and knee
Make my paintings

fun to see!

Foot and Finger Paints

Fingerpaints

YOU'LL NEED:

  ½ cup dry laundry starch

  ½ cup mild soap powder

 ½ to ¾ cup water

food colors

  beater

bowl

WHAT TO DO:

1. Combine starch, soap powder and water.

2. Beat mixture with rotary beater until thick.

3. Add food color to all or part of mixture.

4. Use finger paints on glossy paper, shelf paper or to make letters on hands, feet, arms, legs and so on.

Soap crayons

YOU'LL NEED:

 ¼ cup water

 1 scant cup mild soap powder

food colors

 plastic ice cube tray

plastic wrap

WHAT TO DO:

1. Add soap to ¼ cup water in measuring cup.

2. Stir well. It should be a thick paste.

3. Add 50 drops of food color (or divide in half and make two colors)

4. Mix well. Spoon mixture into section of ice cube tray which you've lined with a sheet of plastic wrap.

5. Let dry overnight.

6. To use: moisten with water, draw letters on arms and legs.

Footpaints

YOU'LL NEED:

 ½ cup flour

 1 cup cornstarch

   2½ cups water

¼ tsp. baking soda

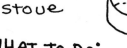 food colors

saucepan

stove

WHAT TO DO:

1. Mix flour and cornstarch.

2. Add water and mix.

3. Cook and stir until thickened and transparent.

4. Add more water (if necessary) to keep mixture creamy and not too thick.

5. Cool. Knead in baking soda and color.

6. Have children sit on low chairs and 'draw' with their toes and feet on paper.

Follow-up Activities

Body Painting

Using the paints, have each child write an H on their own hand, F on their foot, and so on. In the warm weather, have them write a B on each other's backs, K's on their knees, E on their elbows. Let children run through the sprinkler or wash off in a wading pool.

Fingerpainting Fun

Have children:
• Practice drawing letters with the fingers as a brush
• Fingerpaint directly on a table top. Place paper over the painting, smooth slightly, and pull up for a one-of-a-kind finger painting.
• Try fingerpainting letters with the side of their hand, with knuckles, with elbow, the heel of their hand, their fist, and forearm.

Thumb Prints

• Have children stamp thumb prints to create letters . Use a styrofoam tray covered with layers of paper towels Towels act as a stamp pad when tempera paint is poured on top of them. Have each child put thumb into the paint tray and stamp out a thumb print in the shape of a letter. Children might also fill in a block letter with different colored prints.

Finger Letters

Try making finger letters for the children to imitate or guess. You'll need to use both hands to make one letter and please note that B, N, and R are perhaps too difficult to make.

Body Letters

• Draw the shape of a large letter on a sheet of cardboard and ask the children to lie on it in that shape.
• Have the children use their bodies to make the shape of the letter lying down and/or standing up.
• Use masking tape to make a letter. Have children walk , tip toe, take giant steps, and crawl on it .

Alphabet Actions

• After making the body letters, ask one child to move like something that begins with that letter and have everyone guess. You might have to help with some suggestions. For example, make a letter A and then, move like an airplane or an ape. You can also give a child either a picture of an object or just a letter (This is harder.) and have him act out the object or any object that begins with that letter. The others must guess first what the object is and then what the letter is.
• Call out a letter and tell children to touch the part of their body that starts with the letter E (ear, elbow, eye), T (tooth, toe, tummy), A (arm), H (hand, hair), N (neck, nail , nose), F (finger, forehead), M (mouth), L(leg).

Mouth Letters

Tell children to watch your lips carefully while you mouth a letter. Have them guess which one it is. Let them mouth letters for you and classmates to guess.

Air Letters

Using finger movements in the air, have children make letters for the rest of the class to guess.

Flashlight Letters

Using his arm muscles and movements, have one child draw light letters with a flashlight on the blackboard or other dark surface for the other children to guess.

Water Letters

Using a paintbrush, bucket, water, and the chalkboard, have children draw water letters and then,wash the board clean!
• For a real child-pleaser on a nice sunny day, take a portable chalkboard outside to your yard and have children shoot alphabet letters onto the board with water pistols.

Giant Blocks

Once upon a time, there was a mother and father giant. They were good kind people. So when they had a baby, he was the sweetest baby giant in the whole world! Mama and Papa Giant used an old train car for his cradle and put him out in the pasture to play as if he were in a playpen. He would crawl around and play hide-and-seek with the cows. The little human people (Oh, they were just as big as you and me. But next to the Giant family, they were little-sized people!) waved to the baby and tickled his feet as he giggled and cooed.

As Baby Giant grew a little older, Mama and Papa wondered how they could teach him the letters.

"*Well,*" said Papa, "*we could cut down trees and make letters with them or we could dig rivers in the shape of a letter or we could trace letters in the clouds.*"

But Mama Giant thought that perhaps there was an easier way.

One day, Mama Giant watched as a sturdy, cardboard box was delivered to the house of one of the little human people. The people loved the washing machine that was inside the box, but they just threw the box into the trash heap.

"*What a waste,*" said Mama. Then, she had an idea. She combed the countryside far and wide and collected all the large boxes she could find in the trash heaps. She went to work on them—cutting and painting— and then carried them home.

"*Baby Giant,*" she called. "*Look at the surprise I have for you.*" She handed the boxes to her son. Each box had a letter cut out of it and had pictures all around that started with the same letter's sound. Mama Giant had made a set of alphabet blocks for her giant baby!

GIANT BLOCKS

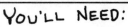

YOU'LL NEED:

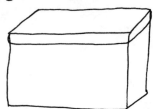

a large carton

plastic type

craft knife

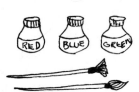

paints and brushes

WHAT TO DO:

1. Using a craft knife, adult cuts out the outline of a large letter that has been traced onto one side. Plastic tape can be added around cut edge to reinforce the opening.

2. Children paint box a solid color, coordinating the letter with the initial letter sound of the color—where possible. G=green

3. Children brainstorm words that start with that letter and paint pictures of these things all around box.

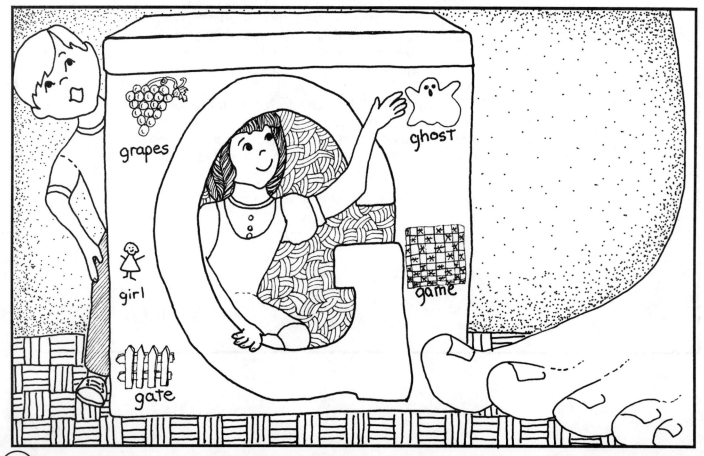

grapes

ghost

girl

game

gate

40

Follow-up Activities

Letter Fishing

Attach paper clips to the backs of paper letters. Using a stick with a string and magnet, have children "fish" for letters in the alphabet pond and identify each one they catch.

Letter Place Card Game

Have each child make a letter place card of their initial and stand it up at their place at the worktable or at the snack table. Mix them all up and see how quickly children can find their seats.

Letter Chain

Help children accordian-fold a piece of paper and draw a letter making sure the edges of the letter go to the edges of the folds. Have them cut out the letter, being careful not to cut on folds. When they unfold it, children will have a lovely decoration.

Carbon Paper Letters

Give children carbon paper and two sheets of paper. Show them how to write a letter on one sheet so that it comes out on the other. Let them practice. Their fascination with the reproduction keeps them going! You can also make your own carbon paper by crayoning over the entire surface of a sheet of paper. Put that paper, crayon side down, over another piece of paper and when you write on it, the crayon image will transfer to the other paper.

All About Me Letter

Give each of the children a large cut-out cardboard letter of their own initial. Tell them to draw and color anything that they like or that makes them feel good onto their letter. Have each child hold up the finished letter and using the letter as a starting point in the following format. *"L my name is Leah and I like . . ."*

Feel and Guess

Put a cut-out cardboard letter in an envelope. Give it to a child. Before it is opened, encourage the child to guess what letter is inside by the way that it feels.

Foil Print

Have children place a cardboard letter under a piece of aluminum foil. Have them rub it with a hand to get an embossed letter. Try using textured papers, such as doilies and sandpaper, to make the cut-out letter placing them under the foil to get a varied textured effect.

Modified Paper Mache Letter

Cut an eight-inch letter from corrugated cardboard. Have children add layers of newspaper or tissue paper strips dipped into liquid starch or glue. This attractive chunky letter can be worn as a necklace, used as a room decoration, or attached to metal bookends to hold up books.

Alphabet Box

Tape a large class-decorated letter (of the week) onto the top of a cardboard box. Encourage children to add small things to the box that begin with that letter. On Friday, share what is inside.

Sign Making Center

Cut out sign shapes and individual letters. Put the letters into a box and encourage children to glue the letters onto the sign to make one that looks like the signs you are studying. Use this in conjunction with a theme that involves the use of signs such as the city, transportation, food, and so on. Signs can be copied from pictures, books, and posters that are in the sign-making center. Use the signs in the dramatic play and block-building corners.

Letter Dominoes

Make letter dominoes out of index cards. Drawn a line down the middle of each and write one letter on each side. Have children play the same way they would with a regular dominoes game---matching letters instead of dots.

Hard/Soft Letters

CHANGES, CHANGES

Changes, changes
Everything rearranges
The rain makes dirt into squishy mud;
The sun makes a seed into a flowering bud.
The wind blows dandelion seeds about;
The spring comes each year and makes new grass sprout.

Changes, changes
Everything rearranges
The caterpillar turns into a butterfly;
The poliwog grows into a frog, bye and bye.
A bird hatches from the tiny egg in the nest;
Autumn leaves fall from trees that need a long winter's rest.

Changes, changes
Everything rearranges
Changes happen in different ways;
Some just come with time and I have no say.
But many changes I can make
Arranging the things I add and take.

Changes, changes
Everything rearranges
I also change each day and year
I grow taller and smarter and have no fear
'Cause change is what happens to all living things
I'm excited and ready for whatever life brings!

Changes, changes
Everything rearranges

HARD/SOFT letters

YOU'LL NEED:

 1 cup water

1 cup Flour

   Food colors

 bowls

bag of cotton balls or cosmetic puffs

 wooden plaque (optional)

glue

 cardboard (optional)

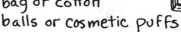 greased baking sheet

WHAT TO DO:

1. Adult or child combines flour and water in bowl and stirs until mixture is smooth. Divide mixture into three bowls equally.

2. Add food coloring to each bowl. Make one bowl red, one yellow and one green. Mix contents of each bowl well.

3. Child dips a cotton ball into one bowl and turns it until the entire ball is covered with mixture. Do not squeeze ball!

4. Place many dipped balls on lightly greased baking sheet to form a letter. Make sure each ball touches the one next to it.

5. Bake in a 300°F oven for one hour or until lightly browned and hard. Let cool on the baking sheet.

6. Letters can be used as is, or mounted on cardboard or on a wooden plaque.

Follow-up Activities

Cotton Ball Toss

With a marker, divide a shirt box bottom into 26 drawn divisions and label each one with a different letter from A to Z. Put one cotton ball into the box. Have a child toss it into the air. Have her catch it in the box. Encourage the child to identify the letter where the cotton ball lands.

Popcorn Sculptures

Popcorn has a hard/soft quality about it. The unpopped kernels are hard. The popped corn is pliable and softer to the taste and touch. Make popcorn letter sculptures.
You'll Need:
- 1/2 cup corn kernels
- 1 cup honey
- 2 tablespoons butter

What to Do:
1. Pop kernels and place in a bowl.
2. In a saucepan, boil one cup honey and two tablespoons of butter until mixture reaches 270 degrees F on a candy thermometer.
3. Remove from heat and add a teaspoon of vanilla. Pour hot syrup onto popcorn and mix well.
4. Cool until it can be handled.
5. Have children pick up popcorn and shape into large letters, buttering hands as needed to keep it from sticking. Set on waxed paper to dry.

Name Bingo

Play with three to five children. Write each child's name, fairly large, on a cash register tape with a marker. Give child this paper and several cotton balls. Write all the letters needed to make sure each child's name can be spelled on little slips of paper. Select one of these letter slips and show it to children. Direct them to use a cotton ball to cover that letter, if it appears in their name. Tell them to call out "Bingo" when all the letters in their name have been called and covered. Use full names or nicknames so that each child's name is approximately the same length. Plan it so that when you are selecting letters to call out, you make sure that each child reaches the Bingo stage at about the same time.

"I" Puppets

I AM : A MINI PLAY

This is a short play about the character I-am. The play tells how I-am found himself. It incorporates the use of the puppets made on the following page.

CAST OF CHARACTERS:
I-am-the-Smartest
I-am-the-Best
I-am-the-Handsomest
I-am-the-Richest
I-am
the boss
the twin i's
the friend
the neighbor
the narrator

SETTING : small town about 50 miles south of here

NARRATOR: Our play opens with the I's standing around the center of town talking to each other.

I-AM-THE-SMARTEST: I am the smartest person in the whole world.

I-AM-THE-BEST : I am the best. I can do anything!

I-AM THE HANDSOMEST : I am the most handsome person in the whole world.

I-AM-THE-RICHEST : I am the richest person in the world.

I-AM : And I am. . I am . . ..

NARRATOR : But I-AM couldn't finish the sentence.

I-AM-THE-SMARTEST : Ha, ha! Ask me any question. I know all the answers!

I-AM-THE-BEST : Let's race or play a game, 'cause I can do anything better than you!

I-AM-THE-HANDSOMEST : I am just so-o-o gorgeous,   especially compared to you.

I-AM-THE-RICHEST : Well, I have lots of money and can buy anything!

NARRATOR : I-AM felt very sad because he didn't know what or who he was. All he knew was that he was NOT the smartest and NOT the best and NOT the handsomest and that he had only a little money. So while the others spent all their time showing off, I-AM spent his time working hard at his job, playing with his two little i twin sons or talking with his friend and helping his neighbor paint the house.

BOSS : I-AM, you are a very good worker.

TWIN i's : Daddy, you are the greatest.

FRIEND :   I-AM, you are a true friend.

NEIGHBOR : I-AM, you are a good helper.

NARRATOR : Suddenly I-AM realized that he was all those things. He was a good and kind person. He also knew that he was probably not the best at everything, of course. But he cared about others, not just himself, and he knew that
was what counted.

I-AM : Now I know who I am . I'm ME and I like Me!

"I" PUPPETS

YOU'LL NEED:

a coat hanger

old nylon stocking

scrap paper

masking Tape

twist tie

glue

scissors

WHAT TO DO:

1. Child, with adult's help, stretches and bends a coat hanger into a rectangular shape with the hook bent together as a handle.

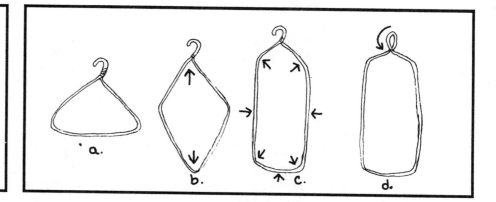

a.

b.

c.

d.

2. The piece of old nylon stocking is stretched and pulled over the hanger and secured, with a twist tie, at the loop handle.

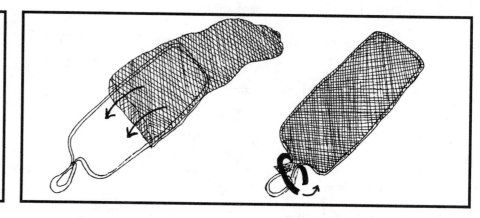

3. Handle is covered with several layers of masking Tape. Eyes, nose and mouth are cut from paper and glued onto stocking.

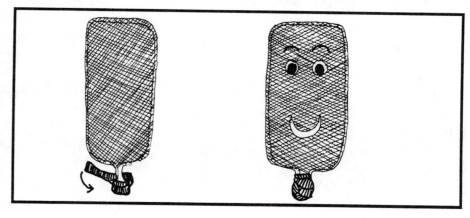

Follow-up Activities

"Stained Glass" Letter

Grate old crayons on a cheese grater (The grater can then be cleaned by pouring boiling water over it.) until you have many colored crayon shavings. Let children sprinkle shavings on a piece of wax paper. Cover it with another piece of wax paper and top it with a piece of plain paper. Iron on top of plain paper until crayon shavings melt. Remove plain paper. Help each child trace and cut out a large letter from the wax paper pieces. Punch a hole in the top of each letter, string, and hang in a window.

Surprise Letter Etching

With thick yellow crayon, draw or have children draw block letters randomly on a sheet of construction paper, surrounded with patches of other crayoned colors, such as red and blue. Cover everything with thick black crayon. Have children scratch away the black with the edges of paper clips until they can identify the letters that appear.

Letter Rubbings

Take children on a Letter Rubbing Walk. With just crayons and paper, they can make rubbings of letters that they find on the walk. They can find letters on manhole covers, license plates, engraved signs, tombstones, and building cornerstones. Have children cover the letters with paper and rub with the side of crayons until the letters appear.

Glitter Letter

Let children crayon a letter onto sandpaper. Then, melt it in the oven at 250 degrees F for three to four minutes and the children will have a glittery, shiny letter painting.

Rainbow Letters

Arrange crayons in a rainbow fashion (R, O, Y, G, B , P). Place another crayon behind these six and perpendicular to them. Secure with rubber band in a figure-eight pattern across front. Have children use the six attached crayons to draw a letter. When it is drawn, it will look like a rainbow.

Jiggling Letters

THE   JIGGLE DANCE
(*Chant words.*)

Jiggle and wiggle and

(*children wiggle and jiggle*)

Jump, jump, jump.

Wobble and bobble and   (*children wobble side to*
        Bump, bump, bump.   side and bob up*
and   *and down and*
bump   *hips*)
 Shake, shake, shake   (*children shake their bodies*
      Shake,   *and turn around*)
Twirl and roll.

 Take, take, take   (*children make grabbing*
Some   *motions*)
 Jelly in a bowl.

Keep it movin'   (*children dance around*)
Keep it groovin'
Jelly needs no improvin'.

So-o-o, be a stretchy E   (*children form one leg*
Dance into a C   *and two arms into*
Whirl around to P   *an E, bend*
and collapse in a D   *into a C, and then*
Wiggily,   *form a P and*
Finally !   *collapse to ground*
                                 wiggling into a D)

JIGGLING LETTERS

YOU'LL NEED:

ORANGE — ORANGE
2 pkg. flavored gelatin

3 tblsp. unflavored gelatin

8"x8" or 9"x9" pan

1 cup water

2 cups boiling water

2 bowls

spatula
plastic knife
spoon

WHAT TO DO:

1. Adult prepares gelatin with help of children. First, put 3 tblsp. unflavored gelatin in one cup cold water. Mix very well.

2. Child puts 2 pkgs. flavored gelatin in large bowl. Adult adds 2 cups boiling water and mixes.

3. Child adds plain gelatin to flavored gelatin and stirs until all is dissolved.

4. Adult pours into pan and refrigerates to set. (20 minutes to 1 hour.)

5. Remove solid piece of gelatin from pan with spatula. Cut letter with paper pattern and table knife or...

6. Use cookie cutters to cut out gelatin. Let the gelatin wiggle and jiggle and then eat!

Follow-up Activities

Jewels in a Cloud

After the letters are all cut out, make a treat from the leftover scrap gelatin. Place it in a big bowl. Have children add whipped cream, Cool Whip, or other substitute. Stir gently so that the gelatin is concealed inside the cream and then, watch children find and enjoy the jewels.

Letter Sticker/Stamps (with jello glue)

Place a teaspoon of flavored gelatin powder and two teaspoons of water in a small saucepan and stir well. Cook until dissolved. Cool slightly and let children brush this glue on the back of cut-out paper or magazine letters. Place on a sheet of wax paper to dry thoroughly. These can be stored on wax paper until ready to use. When moistened with a wet sponge, they will stick like stamps.

Scented Letters

Prepare the gelatin with half the amount of water directed on the package. While it is still in the liquid state, let children paint letters on typing paper, using new brushes or food brushes. Use several diffferent colors--red, orange, and yellow. When dried, have children smell the letters and tell which letter smells like orange or what the red O smells like.

Kitchen Sculpture

boxes
brushes
rocks   roller skates
and   from two old
rings   and wheels
gift wrap   grates
twigs   iron
foam   plates
and   paper
strings
bottles   safety
cups   pins
blocks   old
and comb   swim fins
trash   rusty
scraps   crusty
discards   cupcake
found   tins
around
home

Just a pile of JUNK, you say?
Look again! It's a sculptured K !

KITCHEN SCULPTURE

YOU'LL NEED:

 paper goods
 corks
 egg cartons
 bottle caps

kitchen scrap materials

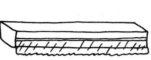 **waxed paper**

 tacky white glue

 ball point pen

SCRAP BOX

WHAT TO DO:

 1. Adult assembles kitchen scrap materials and demonstrates how items can be put together to construct a letter. Allow children to play with materials.

 2. With ball point pen, adult etches a large outline of a letter on waxed paper. Children use glue to construct letter from scrap items over etched letter.

3. Let sculpture dry overnight on waxed paper. Peel paper away from letter the next day. Reglue any loose parts.

Follow-up Activities

A "Dear Parent" Letter

Many of the letter crafts, suggested throughout this book, can be made with items found around our homes. Send the following "Save Your Junk" letter to your children's parents with a list of the *items that they should save and bring in to school.*

Dear Parents,
We will be making many exciting projects this year from simple items that we all use in our homes. Please help us by saving them and sending them into class with your child. We are sure that you will be surprised and delighted at their transformation when your child brings his or her projects home. Please save and send:
- *Bottle caps*
- *Empty spools*
- *Paper cups*
- *Plastic lids*
- *Foam from old cushions or pillows*
- *Old , broken, or unused elephones or typewriters*
- *Spray bottles*
- *Styrofoam trays*
- *Styrofoam packaging pieces*
- *Carbon paper*
- *Shoe boxes*
- *Shirt boxes*
- *Buttons*
- *Used stamps*
- *Telephone wire*
- *Egg cartons*
- *Yarn*
- *Inner tire tube rubber*
- *Aluminum foil pie plates*
- *White pillow cases*

Thank you.
Your Child's Teacher

Telephone Letters

Use an old discarded telephone to talk about letters. Ask children which ones are missing? (Q and Z) Help children spell out their names in a number code.

Lullaby Dream Pillow

(First, read the story to your children, perhaps at naptime. Then, read the story again, another day, and have children listen for all the L's in the story. They can hold up a paper L every time they hear a word that begins with the letter!)

THE SWEETEST LULLABY IN THE WORLD

Once upon a time long ago, in the town of Loud, lived children who hated to take naps. After lunch each day, they loudly protested that they would not take a nap! Just as loud, their parents would tell them to sleep. So each afternoon, you could hear shouts and loud voices arguing, while the children grew tired and grouchy and the parents grew angrier and angrier.

One day, a lively Leprechaun came to the town of Loud. Everyone looked at him in surprise. They knew that Leprechauns were a little magical and rarely did people see them.

But the people of Loud had an idea.

"Let's ask the Leprechaun to help make our children take naps," they shouted.

"Oh, Leprecaun, please help us to get our children to take a nap each day. They grow so tired after lunch, but will not sleep," they bellowed to the small fellow.

The Leprechaun's ears wiggled as he listened to the loud request made by the people.

"Yes, " he softly said ,"I will help you, but I must ask one thing in return."

"Anything at all, they all hollered back at him.

The Leprechaun looked up at them and said quietly,"I want to hear the sweetest lullaby in the whole world."

The townspeople clamored loudly to each other and then said," Of course, that will be easy."

So the Leprechaun gathered all the children, and with the parents following, he took them down to the lake. Of course, it sounded like a parade as they laughed and played Leap Frog along the way.

At the lake, the Leprechaun pointed out flowers and plants that grew along the edge. The children picked lillies, lavender, and lemon-scented leaves. Then, they all followed (again making much noise) the Leprecaun back to town and watched as he quickly, as if by magic, sewed up a tiny, sweet dream pillow , stuffed with the lovely leaves and flowers they had picked, for each child.

The Leprechaun handed out all the pillows and exclaimed,"Now, I want to hear the sweetest lullaby in the world!"

The children lay down with their heads on their pillows and the parents began to speak loudly to each other.

"I will sing the sweetest lullaby," said one woman," I have 10 children and know quite a bit about lullabies."

She sang a lullaby very loudly. It was nice, but the Leprechaun was not impressed.

"I will sing the sweetest lullaby," yelled one man. "I am the lead singer at church."

He sang a lullaby very nicely and, of course, very loudly.

Still the Leprechaun was not impressed and the children grew restless. "No more," he exclaimed "I want to have QUIET!"

Suddenly, there was not a sound coming from anyone in the Land of Loud. It was quiet. Then, in the silence could be heard the sound of a lark calling to its mate who answered back with another sweet call. The sound of the winds whispering through the pines could also be heard. Even the croak of the bull frogs made a happy rhythm along with the katydids' buzz and the humming of bees.

"That is the sweetest lullaby in the whole world," whispered the Leprechaun. But no one heard him for the children were fast asleep on their pillows and the parents were napping right along side of them.

LULLABY DREAM PILLOW

YOU'LL NEED:

calico or muslin fabric · polyester stuffing · potpourri · scissors · needle/thread · sewing machine (optional) · marker · piece (6"x8") of cardboard

WHAT TO DO:

1. Adult cuts two pieces of fabric: each piece is 8"x10". Place right sides of fabric together.

2. Child or adult hand sews (or adult machine sews) the two pieces together ½" in from edges on 3 sides of pillow.

3. Adult clips corners of sewn pillow and child turns pillow right side out.

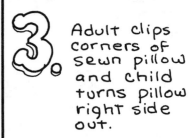

4. Slip cardboard into pillow and have children write their initials on the center of their pillows in marker.

5. Remove cardboard. Stuff firmly with polyester stuffing and small amount of potpourri

6. Adult uses a slip stitch to close pillow.

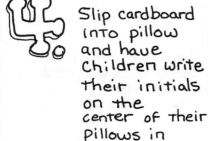

Follow-up Activities

Markers

Help children use markers (Be sure to check the directions on each type of marker.) to write on or add initials to:
- Mugs
- Dishes
- Fabrics (clothing, pillows, hats)
- Papers

Dress-up a Letter

Give each child a block letter and a variety of colored markers. Have the class "dress up" the letter with designs, shapes, faces, or clothes. When they are finished, play a guessing game with the letter designs; for example, " *I'm thinking of one of these letters that is dressed up in* orange curls. *Can you guess which letter that is?*"

Balloon Release

With markers, write one large letter of the alphabet on blown up balloons. Place in a large plastic garbage bag. Release all the balloons and ask each child to catch one and tell you which letter she caught. If you can use helium balloons, tie long strings to them, release in the room, and have children jump to catch a string, bring the balloon down, read the letter, and release for another child to try.

Musical Stepping Stones

Write one letter on each of 26 sheets of paper. Place them on the floor so that children can walk, hop, or jump sequentially on them.

ABC Stepping Stones

Use the same 26 sheets of paper as you did in ABC Stepping Stones (above). This time, have children dance around the letters while you play music. When the music stops, have children go to a stepping stone. They are safe, if they can tell you the name of the letter on which they are standing.

Alphabet in the Dell

Make 26 cards each with a letter and one object starting with that letter of the alphabet drawn or pasted on. Place the cards in the center of your circle. Sing this song to the tune of the *"Farmer in the Dell." "The Farmer takes an A..."* and *"The A takes the B....,"* having each child take the part of one letter. When a child is chosen to be a letter, she has to find the object card in the middle of the circle, hold it up, then join the chain of children singing. At the end of the song, have each child identify the object on her card.

Letter/Color Sort

Give a big block letter drawn on paper to each child. Let each child choose one color marker and fill in the letter with that color. Now, sort all of the letters according to color and make a graph according to color.

Acetate Board

Make a "Write-on/Wipe-off" board from one 9"X12" (approximately) sheet of clear acetate (available in art stores), an exactly-the-same-size piece of corrugated cardboard, and masking tape.

Tape the acetate sheet to the cardboard backing at one 9" long edge. Now, you can draw games and puzzles on an 8 1/2" X 11" piece of paper, slip it under the acetate, and have children play the games by writing with WATER SOLUBLE markers directly on the acetate. Wipe clean with a damp tissue and reuse. Some suggestions for games are:
- Letter completion
- Match the letters
- Match the letter to its object
- Make letter creatures
- Fill in letters in a missing alphabet sequence
- Match capital letters with small letters

Marvelous Munchible Letters

MARVIN'S MARVELOUS MAGICAL M

One day, all the children in Marvin's class were making bread dough letters . After they shaped the letters, the bread dough would be put into the oven to bake . Everyone made big, beautiful letters--everyone except Marvin, that is. Marvin's M looked awful. It was too skinny in parts and too fat in other parts. And, it even had holes in it! The other children laughed at the crooked M. Poor Marvin was very upset because, as hard as he tried, he just couldn't make a good bread dough M.

"Ha,ha," laughed Billy. "Marvin made the funniest looking M I've ever seen!"

"You made an ugly M ," giggled Sally.

Marvin was about ready to cry when suddenly, he saw his bread dough M move! Marvin couldn't believe his eyes!

The large M stood up on the table straight and tall. Marvin, Billy, and Sally just watched it with wide eyes and open mouths. Then, the M changed into an O and rolled right off the table, past the children, and out the door!

"Help, stop my M or O or whatever I made out of bread dough," called Marvin as all the children and teachers followed him out the door.

They chased the rolling O as it passed a woman who cried, "Save my kitten. He's stuck up in this tree".

The O slowed down , stopped, rolled back to the tree and as if by magic, changed its shape into a large letter L. It leaned against the tree and looked like a ladder. The kitten used the bread dough L ladder to climb down and jumped into the woman's arms.

"Thank you," she shouted as the bread dough L changed into a giant H and hopped on down the road. Marvin, the teachers, and the children kept running after the hopping H.

Soon, the H came to a young girl who was crying.

"Oh, I've dropped my quarter into the storm drain and I can't get it out," she sobbed.

The H stopped hopping and changed into a long, skinny S that looked just like string. As Marvin, the girl, and everyone else watched, the S went down the storm drain, wrapped around the quarter and pulled it up. The girl smiled with the quarter in her hand and tried to grab the S , but it had already changed into a J and jumped away.

Everyone was growing tired of chasing Marvin's Marvelous Magical M or O or L or H or S or J or whatever letter. They just watched as the bread dough letter changed into a G as it turned the corner.

"Now, what?" yelled Marvin as everyone began to run again.

When they got to the corner, they saw that the bread dough G had saved a puppy from running into the road in front of a car by becoming a gate to close the fence. The owner picked up the puppy and patted the G which already had changed back into the M. When it saw Marvin, the M leaped into Marvin's hands. It gave Marvin a kiss, then turned upside down, and, looking like a W, waved at Marvin and the others and wobbled down the road and out of sight.

Marvin felt a little sad to have lost his marvelous, magical M. But, all the children treated Marvin like a hero, and he went back back to the school and shared plain, but very delicious, baked bread dough letters with everyone!

PEANUT BUTTER PLAY DOUGH

You'll Need:

  1 cup peanut butter

 2/3-1 cup dry milk powder

  3 tblsp. honey

TRIMS (OPTIONAL)

 raisins   seeds   chocolate chips

What To Do:

1. Adult or child mixes peanut butter with honey and dry milk powder until it is the consistency of a stiff, non-sticky play dough. (Add more or less milk powder as needed.

2. Knead 1-2 minutes.

3. Children shape peanut butter play dough into letters.

4. Children can trim letters with raisins, seeds or chocolate chips.

SWEET BREAD DOUGH

You'll Need:

 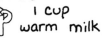 1 cup warm milk

  1/2 cup honey

 2 eggs (beaten)

1/4 cup margarine

 1 tblsp. baking powder

1 tsp. salt

  4 cups Flour

1 egg for glaze

baking sheet

What To Do:

1. Mix together milk, honey and margarine.

2. Add beaten eggs

3. Add dry ingredients, a little at a time.

4. Make a stiff dough. Knead for 5 minutes.

5. Shape dough into letters.

6. Place on lightly greased baking sheet.

7. Glaze with one beaten egg.

8. Bake 15-20 minutes at 350°F.

PRETZELS

You'll Need:

 1½ cups warm water

 1 envelope yeast

 4 cups flour

1 tsp. salt

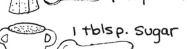 1 tblsp. sugar

 sprinkling of coarse salt

1 beaten egg (glaze)

greased baking sheet

What To Do:

1. Mix together water, yeast and sugar. Set aside for 5 minutes.

2. Put salt and flour in a bowl.

3. Combine yeast mixture and flour mixture. Make a stiff dough.

4. Shape letters from dough right on greased baking sheet.

5. Brush beaten egg over letters and sprinkle with coarse salt.

6. Bake at 425°F for 12 minutes.

Follow-up Activities

Inedible Play Dough Recipes

Most of the inedible play doughs, described below, should be made for children by an adult. They can be stored in a zip-locking bag in the refrigerator for days. Food coloring can be added to the water in these recipes.

Baker's Clay

This dough is best used right away and NOT stored.

You'll Need:
- 4 cups of flour
- 1 cup iodized salt
- 1 1/2--1 3/4 cups of warm water

What to Do:
1. Mix salt and flour well.
2. Add water and mix.
3. Knead eight to ten minutes.
4. Have children mold pieces. (Moisten both pieces of dough when put together.)
5. Bake on greased sheet at 250 degrees F. For 1--2 hours or until hard to the touch.

Cooked Play Dough

You'll Need:
- 1 cup flour
- 1/2 cup salt
- 2 teaspoons cream of tartar
- 1 cup water
- 1 tablespoon oil
- 1 teaspoon food coloring

What to Do:
1. Combine flour, salt, and cream of tartar.
2. Add water, oil, and food coloring.
3. Cook over medium heat until thick. Stir well.
4. Cool slightly and knead smooth.

Modeling Clay

You'll Need:
- 1 cup cornstarch
- 2 cups baking soda
- 1 1/4 cup cold water
- 1 teaspoon food coloring

What to Do:
1. Mix all ingredients in a saucepan.
2. Heat and stir until thick (like mashed potatoes).
3. Knead some food coloring into slightly cooled dough.
4. Have children mold. Air dry.

Modeling Goop

You'll Need:
- 2/3 cup water
- 2 cups salt

- 1/2 cup water
- 1 cup cornstarch

What to Do:

I. Add 2/3 cup water to salt in saucepan.
2. Cook over medium heat for four to five minutes.
3. Mix 1/2 cup water with cornstarch in a separate bowl and stir.
4. Add cornstarch mixture to salt mixture.
5. Return to low heat and stir until smooth.

Sand Play Dough

You'll Need:

- 1 cup sand
- 1/2 cup cornstarch
- 3/4 cup hot water

What to Do:

I. Mix ingredients in saucepan.
2. Cook and stir until thickened.
3. Cool and have children model with it.
4. Dry in sunshine for two to three days.

Poem

ALL THE POSSIBILITIES
What is play dough? Who knows?
Not just flower, but possibly a rose.
Not just salt, but possibly the sea.
Not just water, but possibly a giant E.
Not just mush, but possibly the keys.
That, within the minds of children,
unlock all sorts of possibilities!

Neighborhood Mural

Draw pictures or attach photos of you in your neighborhood. Make sure there are lots of letters all around you.

NEIGHBORHOOD LETTERS

YOU'LL NEED:

a camera

film

photos

large mural paper

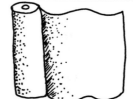
marker

glue

scissors

WHAT TO DO:

 1. Take a photo safari in your local area. Snap pictures of signs: store, traffic, advertising. Try to keep signs in a similar scale.

 2. Take photos of each of your children in outside poses: bike riding, walking doll carriages. Take all photos from same distance.

 3. On large mural paper, adult draws a street scene. It can be your actual street scene.

 4. Draw buildings on your street, and cut out the actual photo signs you took and glue onto mural. Place other signs on mural.

 5. Cut out photos you took of children and place on the street scene where appropriate.

 6. Encourage children to add more drawings to mural and take more photos.

Follow-up Activities

Letter Photo Safari

Take children on a walk in your neighborhood and collect letters on film with a camera. Let them point to letters that they see and help you snap the pictures. When you return to the classroom, have children recall as many of the letters that they saw as they can. Have the film developed as soon as possible so that the photo walk is still fresh in the children's minds. (Many photo shops will develop photos in a few hours or at least by the next day.)

"What Is It?" Poster

Mount your photos from the photo walk onto posterboard. Show the poster to children and see if they can remember in what places those letters were found. Of course, you'll all have to take another walk to see if their answers were correct. (So make sure that you can remember where the letters were seen.)

Mini-"Reward Posters"

Before going on a photo walk, have each child pick or be assigned a specific letter. Then, when you are on the walk and the child finds that letter, take a photo of her with it or in front of it. When you return to class, make a reward poster with the photo, child's name, and the words, "I Found It."

People Alphabet

Have each child hold or wear a letter, preferably the first letter of her name, and take a picture of it. If you do not have enough children to complete the alphabet, ask children to find or suggest other people whose names begin with that letter and take a photo of them for your alphabet. Display your People Alphabet on the wall from A--Z..

Alphabet Photo Sun Imprints

Give each child a sheet of photography paper (available in photo shops and some larger discount stores) in a darkened room. Let them quickly place wooden or plastic letters on it as a design. Set in sunlight for a few minutes. Remove letters one at a time to see light-colored images that are left in varying shades. This paper will eventually turn black, if left as is. To create a more permanent alphabet letter picture that the children can take home, treat the prints to a fixing bath for about five minutes. After the fixing, wash the prints in running water for about 10 minutes and then, let them dry face up on paper towels.

Overstuffed Letters

THE CLEVER KINGDOM

Once upon a time in a kingdom beyond the sea lived a young, but tired, queen. She was so tired because there were so many decisions to make each day, so she rarely got to rest--or even to eat lunch.

"I need help, " she thought to herself. "But, I need someone who is as wise and as clever as I am to help make these decisions."

The big problem was who could she get. No one in the royal palace was that clever, so the queen had to think of another way to find the most wise and most clever person in her kingdom.

As she walked past her palace print shop, the queen spied letters scattered about. They were large, lovely letters. Suddenly, she had an idea. she gathered all 26 of these letters and went to her office. There, she placed each letter into an envelope and addressed them to the 26 families in her kingdom. She, then, sent the letters through the mail.

When the postman delivered the letters, each person opened his envelope and just stared at the alphabet letter. The villagers gathered together and all began to guess who might have sent them and what they were for. But no one really knew. So each of the villagers took his letter home.

"It's lovely," declared several of the wives.

"It's attractive," said others.

"It's fun," announced some of the children.

So each letter was placed in a prominent place in the tiny homes. The D was put on a birdcage for a door. The P was a pull on a window shade. The C was placed as a cushion on a couch. The M swung from the ceiling as a mobile. Two children used the T as a toy. Each village family used the letter in some very clever way.

After a few days, the queen made unannounced visits to each of her 26 villagers' homes. She was amazed to see what each had done with the letter she had mailed to them. She saw that the L was now a lamp, the B was a bonnet, and the E had become an earring!

"What clever subjects I have," she stated. "I sent each of you a letter to see who would use it in the cleverest way. But I now see that I have 26 clever families in my kingdom. Therefore, I shall ask all of you to help me make decisions from now on. "

And, from that day on, that kingdom has always been ruled by all the people with a good and wise queen as their leader.

(Teachers: send a letter of the alphabet home to each of your students. Ask them what clever way they used the letter.)

OVERSTUFFED LETTERS

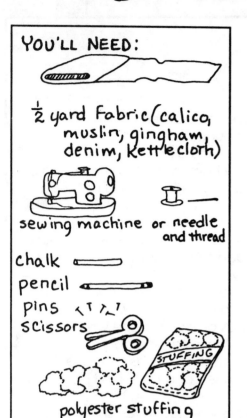

YOU'LL NEED:

½ yard Fabric (calico, muslin, gingham, denim, kettle cloth)

sewing machine or needle and thread

chalk

pencil

pins

scissors

polyester stuffing

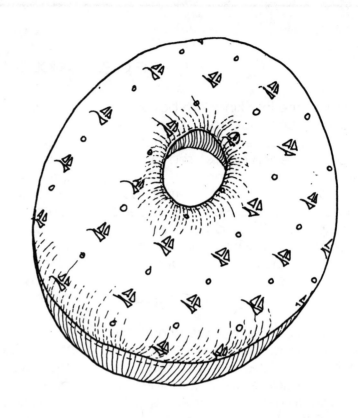

WHAT TO DO:

1. Adult doubles the Fabric, with right sides together, then traces a 10"x14" Tall letter on the wrong side of Fabric with chalk.

2. Adult keeps two fabric pieces together and cuts out the traced letter. You will have two pieces.

3. Keeping fabric together with pins, adult or child stitches ½" in from all outer edges of Fabric. Leave 4" open near bottom.

4. Clip into all curves. Clip tips from any corners. Turn right side out.

5. Adult or child Stitches letter together (on right side) in negative spaces (as in the A, B, D, O, P, Q, R). Clip away material inside sewn area.

6. Stuff letter very tightly with polyester stuffing. Use the eraser side of a pencil to push stuffing into corners. Adult slip stitches pillow closed.

Follow-up Activities

Bean Bags

Letters from the craft on page 72 can be scaled down in size to make bean bags. Have children fill them with dried beans, unpopped popcorn, or bird seed. You can also make square bean bags out of fabric and mark a letter on each.

Foot Toss

Draw a bullseye type of circle with chalk on the sidewalk or in the play yard or inside on the floor or rug. Label the bullseye with letters. Have children sit on chairs in a circle around the outside of the bullseye. Have one child place a bean bag on her foot and toss it onto the bullseye. Direct her to say the name of the letter that the bean bag lands on . Pass the bean bag to the next player.

Bean Bag Scatter

Scatter bean bags with a letter printed on each (or use the letter bean bags) around a small playing area. Have one child pick up as many bean bags as she can in 10 seconds, calling out the name of each letter as it is picked up. Have the rest of the children slowly count to ten. Then, let the child who has picked up the bean bags rescatter them for someone else to pick up.

Swing and Throw

Draw one large letter on a paper plate. Make several of these with different letters. Punch a hole at the top and string with yarn. Tape the yarn ends to the top of the inside of a door frame so the paper plates swing freely and at slightly different heights. Let one child at a time throw the bean bags from a distance of about four to five feet. Have the child name each letter as she hits the plate.

Ladder Toss

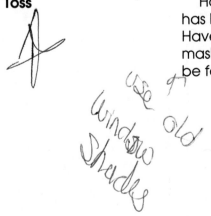

use old
window
shades

Have a child toss a bean bag onto an alphabet ladder that has been drawn with chalk on the sidewalk or in the play yard. Have the child name the letter it lands on. You could also use masking tape to make a ladder on a garbage bag which can be folded, put away, and reused.

Pasta Letters

PRINCE PETER FINDS HIS PRINCESS

Once upon a time there was a village called Pastaville. It was ruled by a gentle and kind family, who had a son named Peter.

One day, Prince Peter asked his wise father, the king, how he should find a girl to marry to become his Princess.

"Son, we are Pasta people and when you find a woman who loves pasta as much as you do, then, you will find your princess."

The prince thought about those wise words but he still didn't know what to do. EVERYONE in Pastaville loved pasta. They ate spaghetti, macaroni, lasagne, and even chicken noodle soup. Now, thinking about soup gave Peter an idea.

"I declare that for one week, no one in Pastaville will be allowed to eat pasta in any way, shape, or form or they will be banished from the village."

"Also,"declared Prince Peter," each lunch and dinner time, I will ask one of the single, eligible girls of the village to dine with me."

So during the next week, no one ate pasta and the Prince invited all the single, eligible girls to dine, one at a time, at the castle with him. Soup was served at each meal, but the Prince had still not found one woman that he wanted for his Princess.

Well, it was the last day of the week, the very last meal with the very last single, eligible girl. Her name was Priscilla. She sat with the Prince at dinner and began to taste the soup. She took one spoonful, put down the spoon, and stared at the prince.

The prince looked startled.

"What is wrong?" he asked.

"I will not eat this soup," declared Priscilla.

A gentle smile came to the prince's face.

"Why not," he asked.

"Because this soup has pasta in it. Oh, I can't see it. It must be at the bottom of the pot. But I know it is there, and I will not risk being banished from my beloved Pastaville. I love pasta more than just about anything else, but I will not eat it!"

Prince Peter was overjoyed. He had put one tiny piece of pasta into the soup pot. All the other single, eligible girls had not even tasted it. But Priscilla was so sensitive and loved pasta so much that she knew it was there.

"Priscilla, you love pasta as much as I do. Will you marry me and become Princess Priscilla of Pastaville?"

"Yes," was her simple reply and they lived together in Pastaville happily ever after.

PASTA LETTERS

YOU'LL NEED:

 pasta

 glue

 paper

or

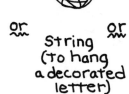 string (to hang a decorated letter)

or

 wooden plaque

WHAT TO DO:

 1. Allow time for children to manipulate pasta and make several letters before giving them glue.

 2. Children choose one letter and form it from pasta on a piece of paper. Pasta pieces are then glued into place to make letter.

 3. Children can use pasta:
- to make names
- to label
- to decorate items.

Pasta can be painted, dyed with food color and glittered.

A PASTA PRIMER

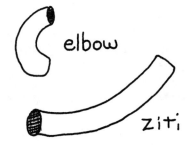

elbow

ziti

seashell

tubetti

 rigatoni

 fusilli

linguine

spaghetti

vermicelli

"Feel-a-Letter" (Collage Letters)

Draw a box-type letter onto a plain piece of cardboard. Have children use glue and any of the following materials to make a raised textured letter that they can feel: sand, shells, buttons, rice, glitter, colored and crushed egg shells, colored scrap papers, used stamps, spices (so that they can also smell the letter), pennies (for a gift), seeds, and/or a combination of materials from your odds-and-ends box.

Labeling

Use letters for labeling. Attach with white glue.

Magnifying Fun

Spread the little pasta letters on a sheet of paper. Give children a magnifying glass and ask them to find certain letters.

Feely Fun

Put the pasta into a box for children to play with. They love to just put their hands into it and feel the texture. (Every once in a while, a child might ask you to identify a letter; but, in general, these letters are too small for little hands to work with.)

Alphabet Vegetable Soup

Prepare this delicious soup together with children.
You'll Need:
- 2 large cans chicken broth
- Carrots, potatoes, onions, parsley, celery
- Herbs--thyme or dill
- 1/2 - 3/4 cup dry alphabet pasta

What to Do:
1. Have children pour cans of chicken broth, as a base, into a large pot.
2. Help them add small cut-up pieces of carrot, potato, onion, few springs of parsley, and celery with a few leaves. Add herbs to taste, such as dill or thyme.
3. Simmer for five minutes and add 1/2 -3/4 cup of dry alphabet pasta.
4. Stir occasionally to make sure that the pasta does not stick to the bottom of the pan. Season to taste with salt and pepper.

Alphabet Soup Game

Have children sit in a circle with one child in the center. Give each of the children in the circle a letter of the alphabet, making sure that there are two of each letter somewhere in the circle. When the child in the center calls out a letter, the two children with that same letter have to try to switch seats before the center child can get to one of their seats. If he does, the child without a seat becomes the center child. The center child can also call out, "*alphabet soup.*" When that happens, everyone in the circle has to switch seats all at once as the center child tries to find an empty one.

Alphabet Soup Picture

Give each child a piece of construction paper, a paper plate bowl, a real paper napkin, a plastic spoon, and a small handful of alphabet soup letters. Let the child glue the bowl to the construction paper placemat, glue the napkin and spoon in place alongside the bowl, and glue the alphabet soup noodles to the inside of the bowl.

Quilt Letter

A Z Y - COLOR - X W V

- CUT -

- MATCH -

Color each patch and cut out on dotted lines.
Match each alphabet letter patch to space on quilt.

B U

C 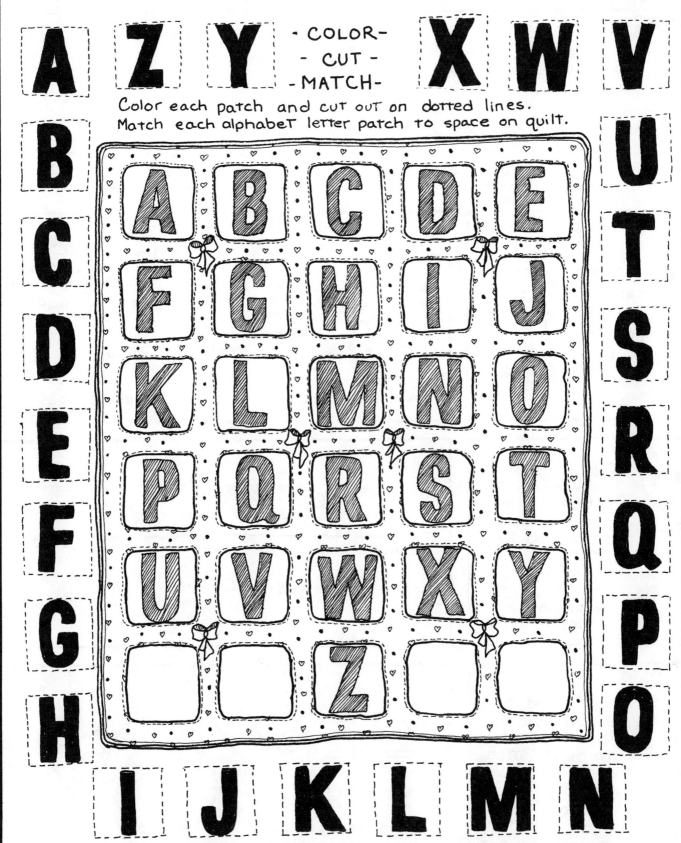 T

D S

E R

F Q

G P

H O

I J K L M N

QUILTED LETTER

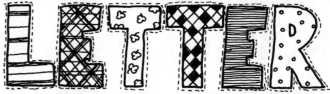

YOU'LL NEED:

²/₃ yd of muslin

batting

choice of material to appy letter:

Fabric

Fabric Crayons

red blue

scissors
pins

permanent
permanent

needle and cotton thread

WHAT TO DO:

1. Child or adult applies a large, block-style letter to a 10" square of muslin.

Use one of the suggested ways.

Ways to Put Letters on Fabric

★ hand applique

★ machine applique

★ permanent markers

★ fabric crayon transferes

★ stenciled fabric paints

2. Adult layers piece of muslin with letter on it over a piece of batting. Both pieces are placed over another piece of muslin. Pin or tape to hold.

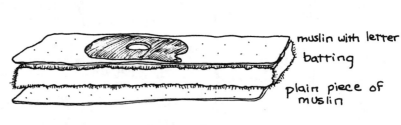

muslin with letter
batting
plain piece of muslin

Layered for Quilting

3. Child or adult uses needle and cotton thread to quilt. Stitch directly up from back fabric through batting to top. Take tiny stitches straight up and down!

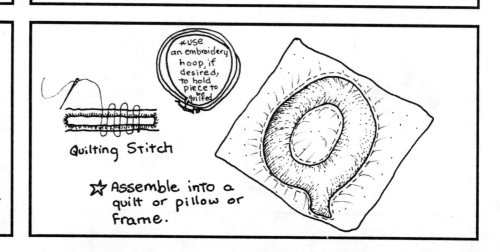

*use an embroidery hoop if desired, to hold piece to be quilted

Quilting Stitch

★ Assemble into a quilt or pillow or frame.

Follow-up Activities

Applique

Here are several quick alphabet quilts to make.
• Draw alphabet letters onto muslin squares with permanent markers instead of appliquing them on. Let each child write her name on the letter square that corresponds with her first initial.
• Use a solid piece of muslin and draw the lines of the squares onto it with permanent markers instead of sewing squares together. Have children use markers, fabric, crayons, appliqued fabric, or glued-on felt to make the letters.
• Make a Burlap and Felt Quilted Wall Hanging. Help children make a quilt using one large piece of burlap (Felt can be used but is much more expensive.) and cut-out felt letters. Yarn can be glued on to make the squares for the quilt.

Initial Pillows

Applique (or draw with permanent markers) the first letter of each child's name onto a 10-inch piece of muslin. Make a pillow out of the letter with another piece of fabric in either muslin or the same material as the letter. Sew the two pieces of fabric together and stuff to make a pillow. Give each child her pillow to use at naptime.

Banner Feltboard

Make a feltboard by wrapping and gluing felt around a piece cardboard that has been cut into the shape of a banner (approximately 18" X 24"). Use this to '"celebrate" your letter of the week with a parade. Each week, have a new parade by replacing the letter on your banner. Have children give three cheers for the letter, rally around it, and then, hang the banner on the door for parents to see.

Rubber Stamps

YOU AND I TOGETHER

(Sing this song to the tune of ' On Top Of Old Smokey'. As you sing this song, let children stamp out the letters mentioned in the song for "you." Then, add the letter mentioned for "I." You will have made a word!

If you had an A,
> along with a P,
> I'd add my own E and we'd swing from a tree.

If you had a T ,
> along with a U,
> I'd add my own G and set sail with you.

If you had a T ,
> along with an O,
> I'd add my own P and spin to and fro.

If you had a C,
> along with an A,
> I'd add my own T and with our pet we would play.

If you had a D,
> along with an O,
> I'd add my own G and for a bone we would go.

If you had an M,
> along with an A,
> I'd add my own P and search for treasure all day.

If you had an E
> and I had two G's,
> We'd put them together and eat omelettes with cheese!

RUBBER STAMPS

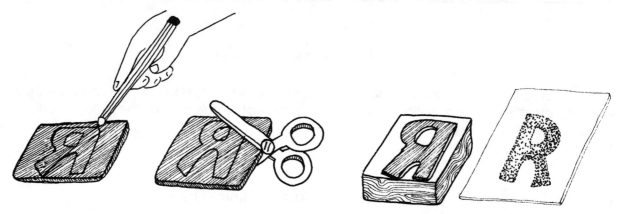

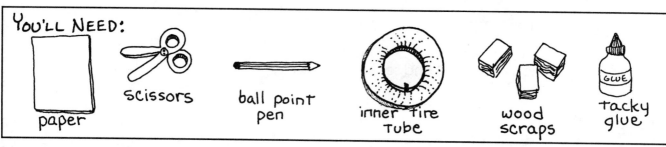

YOU'LL NEED:

paper · scissors · ball point pen · inner tire tube · wood scraps · tacky glue

WHAT TO DO:

 1. Adult or child draws or traces a block letter— of any size— onto a piece of paper.

 **2.** Adult or child cuts out the paper pattern letter with scissors.

 3. Adult uses ball point pen to trace around letter pattern on the inner tire tube rubber.

 **4.** Adult or child cuts out rubber letter with scissors.

 **5.** Adult mounts and glues letter onto wood scrap. Make sure letter is backwards on wood.

 6. Let rubber stamp dry overnight. Use stamp letter with tempera paint or a stamp pad.

Follow-up Activities

Letter Stamps

Use the letter stamps to stamp out letters for labelling, Stamp out the names of objects in the room and attach labels to them.

Patterning

Stamp out a pattern on the top of a piece of paper--EEER-EEER. Have children repeat the pattern underneath it. Encourage them to make up their own patterns.

Hide and Seek

Have one child stamp a letter onto a square of paper. Tell him to find something in the room whose name begins with that letter and put the paper on it. Tell the rest of the class what the letter is and see if they can find and identify the object.

Billboard Mural

To have children become aware of the many uses of letters (and words) on signs, take a class walk, pointing out all of the uses of letters that you see: on traffic signs, billboards , buildings, license plates, and street signs. When you return to your classroom, draw large empty signs (movie, store, traffic,) incorporated into a city scene on a large piece of newsprint that has been rolled out on the floor. Have children fill in the empty signs using their rubber stamps. (They do not have to spell anything.)

Concentration Game

Ask children to stamp one letter onto a cardboard square. Make two sets of all 26 letters. Using only four or five pairs of letters at a time, play Concentration.

Letter Counting

Mark a piece of paper into 10 equal sections. Write a number on the left hand side of each section from 1 to 10. Have children stamp out the corresponding number of letters of their choice in the correct section. This activity may be done with individual children or the group with children taking turns stamping and counting together.

Sand Letters

SAND

(Read this poem to children as they touch sand so that they can 'act out' ' the words)

Tiny little grains
                    of pinks, whites, and tans
Make the lovely seashore
                    full of sparkling sands.
Once mighty rocks and cliffs
                    chipped away by ocean drifts,
Now lie upon the edge of the sea
                    just waiting there for you and me. . .
To dig and dump, push and pile,
To bury our feet for just a while.
To build castles, caves, and moats
                    or hollow out great pretend boats.
But best of all-
                    using just our hands-
We love to write LETTERS in the sands.

All the letters of the alphabet-
                    with names and games
                    and so much more-
Carved along the sandy shore. . .
                    Yet,
With the splash of a rolling wave,
                    our letters cannot be saved.
The Sea wants back what she once gave.
But we never mind,
                    we still have fun,
As water erases
                    the letters we've done .
Now we start over
                    with an "A" or a "B"
And laugh and giggle
                    as letters wash free. . .
                        back again into the sea.

SAND LETTERS

YOU'LL NEED:

 Plaster of Paris

 bucket

 water SAND

 wooden block

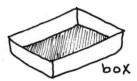 box

WHAT TO DO:

1. Children line box with a sheet of plastic wrap. Moist sand is placed about 2/3 up the sides in the box.

2. Child uses a block to form letter in moistened sand. Make letter 1–1½" deep. Adult prepares plaster as directed.

3. Children immediately pour plaster into letter form. Allow to dry 30 minutes. Remove letter from sand. Brush away excess sand.

Follow-up Activities

Sand Candle Letters

Instead of casting in Plaster of Paris, help children make a sand candle in the shape of a letter. You will need candle wicking and parafin (available in craft stores). Have children shape the letter in the moist sand (You may want to poke a pencil deeper into the sand at three separate points around the letter to make a three-pointed stand on it).

Tie one end of the wick to a pencil and cut the other end a little longer than the formed letter is deep. Lie the pencil and wick across the letter somewhere near the center. Melt parafin in a double boiler pot (or set parafin in a one-pound coffee can and set that into a two-pound coffee can filled partially with water). Never melt parafin directly over heat!

Pour just-melted parafin into sand letter form very carefully making sure hot parafin doesn't splash. Let cool for 1-1 1/2 hours. Ply up candle. Brush off excess sand .

Sand Paper Letters

Trace the letter about 4" high onto pieces of medium weight sandpaper. Child or adult cuts them out, glues and mounts them on posterboard cards.

Colored Sand Names and Initials

Place one cup of white sand in a zip-locking bag with about 10 drops of a food color. Close bag. Vigorously shake the bag until all the sand is colored. Open the bag and spread sand out to dry. Repeat with any color desired. Have children write their names using a large brush with slighted deluted white glue on cardboard. Immediately, have them sprinkle on these colored sands. Let dry, then shake off the excess sand. This makes a spectactular name poster!

Sandpaper Letter Melt

Cut large, block letters from sand paper. Have children decorate each very solidly with crayon placed directly on top of the rough side. Adult places the letter on a cookie sheet and into a 300 degree F oven for four to five minutes or until crayon melts . Letter will emerge in vivid colors!

Sun-baked Sand Dough Letters

Combine one cup of sand with cup of cornstarch and cup of water in a saucepan. Cook over medium heat until mixture is thick. Remove from heat and let cool a few minutes. Then, have children knead a few times.

Have children form letters from sand dough on a flat surface and set outside in the hot sun for a day to "bake."

Sand Collage

Have children go on a beach walk and collect shells, driftwood, and pebbles. Also, bring back a bucket of sand. Cut out large posterboard initials and have children glue down their

beach 'treasures' onto the letter. Have them fill in the empty spaces with sand so the entire letter is covered.

Buried Letters

Have children bury small, plastic (They can be magnetic letters.) letters around in many places in the sandbox. Then, have the same or other children take turns finding one letter with their hands and identifying it while it is still under the sand only by touching it!

If the identification is correct, the child gets to keep the letter. If it is incorrect, the letter is again slipped under the sand to be found once more.

Sand Substitutes--
   Salt, Cornmeal,
   Short grain rice

Although these cannot be used for crafts, they make great substitutes for indoor play where sand is not available or too messy. Children can write letters with their fingers in these materials as well as play and dig.

Letters in Trays

Connect the dots in A B C order. Start at the star.

 A   B   C   D   E   F

Z   •G

                                            •H

Y   X   W   •J   i

        V•   •K

        U•   •L

        T•   •M

        S•   •N

        R•   •O
        Q•   •P

LETTERS IN TRAYS

YOU'LL NEED:

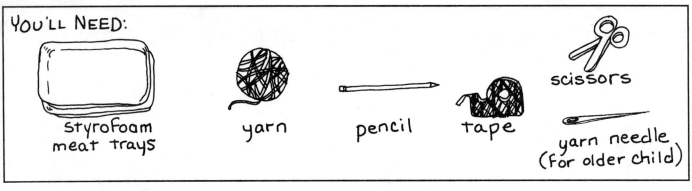

styrofoam meat trays   yarn   pencil   tape   scissors   yarn needle (for older child)

WHAT TO DO:

1. Adult uses a sharp pencil point to poke holes into styrofoam tray in letter shape. Make sure to make an even number of holes.

2. Adult prepares yarn: Cut an 18" length of yarn and tightly tape one end—almost to a point. Knot the other end. Or, use a yarn needle with yarn.

3. Children 'sew' the letter by moving the yarn in and out through the holes. Knot end and cut off excess.

Follow-up Activities

Styrofoam Dig

Fill a box with styrofoam packing pieces. On 52 of those pieces, mark one letter of the alphabet so that there are two sets of the whole alphabet. Let children "dig" for any piece with a letter on it, name it, and keep it.

Foam Tray Printing

Etch a letter into a foam tray with a broken pencil point. (Remember that some letters need to be done backwards). Ink the tray with tempera paint and brush or water-soluble printer's ink and a brayer. Have a child place a sheet of paper over inked or painted surface and rub it with his hand. Have him pull paper up from one corner. Let dry. Repeat process as often as desired using the same tray and new pieces of paper and ink.

Styrofoam Tray Puzzle

Cut a whole letter out of the center of a styrofoam tray. Use additional trays to make more letters. Have children replace the letters in their correct trays.

Tinsmithing Letters

Place an aluminum foil pie plate on a piece of scrap wood. Have children hammer a nail into the plate forming the shape of a letter with the holes.

Paper Punch Decorated Letters

With a hole puncher, have children punch out a letter from a piece of white paper. Have them attach a piece of colored cellophane behind it to create an interesting effect.

Uniform Letters

ALPHABERT

Alphabert loved letters. Although he was only five years old, he could name every letter of the alphabet and sing the "Alphabet Song." He knew A was for apple, and everything all the way to Z for ZIP code.

Everyone knew that Alphabert loved letters, and so, for birthdays, holidays, and sometimes for no reason at all, he got things with letters as gifts. He had letters on his shirts, jackets, hats, and socks. He had letters on his bed, curtains, and towels. He had letters on his toys and on his stuffed animals.

Alphabert was very content. That is, he was until one day when a friend pointed out to Alphabert that he had every letter of the alphabet in his room—all the letters except for one.

Alphabert was very upset! He wanted to have every letter in his room. Can you help Alphabert find which letter is missing? When you decide which letter is missing, draw something in Alphabert's room and write the missing letter on it.

UNIFORM LETTERS

YOU'LL NEED:

sheets of waxed stencil paper

brush(es)

craft knife

ball point pen

paints

item to be stenciled

newspapers magazines

tape

WHAT TO DO:

1. Place waxed stencil paper over letter to be traced. Trace letter onto stencil paper with ball point pen.

2. Adult places stencil paper on an old magazine and uses craft knife to cut out letter.

3. Stencil is now placed on fabric or item to be stenciled and is taped into place. (Place a newspaper under fabric)

4. Child or adult dips brush into small amount of paint. Tap brush on newspaper until paint is worked into brush, but brush tip is almost <u>dry.</u>

5. Stencil by tapping brush straight up and down. Paint should be darkest at stencil edges and very light at center.

6. Let entire stenciled letter dry. If letter is stenciled on fabric, iron on reverse side after 24 hours to set paint.

Follow-up Activities

Stenciling

Children can use their stencils to stencil initials on:
- T-shirts
- Canvas bags
- Pillows rugs
- Blank quilts (See page 80.)
- Brown lunch bags
- Greeting cards
- Wrapping paper.

The inside cut-out letter of the stencil that was just made can be used as a pattern to trace around or in spatter and spray painting.

Sprayed Letters

Fill a spray bottle (from an empty, clean detergent container) with diluted paints. Have children spray onto stencils under which you have placed pieces of paper. Lift stencils to reveal letter shapes.

Negative Painting

Tape the letter pattern (or make a letter shape out of masking tape) onto a sheet of paper. Spatter, spray or dot (using pencil eraser dipped into paint) paint all over the paper. When dry remove the tape and the letter will stand out from the decorated background.

Vegetable Printing

Use any of the following vegetables for printing: potatoes, carrots, squash, or apples. Cut the letter into the flat surface of the vegetable. (Remember that the letter has to be backwards.) Have children dip into poster paint and print! Have them compare the different kinds of prints they can get from the different vegetables.

Chalk Painting

Wet pieces of chalk and draw letters on construction paper with the side of the wet chalk.

Water Painting

Give children a large paintbrush and a bucket of water and have them paint letters on the buildings and sidewalks

Very Soft Bowling

WHAT IF...

What if...
     the world was made of soft foam—
          I mean the ground, the cars, the trees, my home!

What if...
     I ran to play outside
          I would tumble and jounce down my soft foam
slide!

What if...
     each foam flower, kitten, and bug
          Just sprang out of my arms as I gave it a hug!

What if...
     cars rolled 'round on rubber tires
          Then, firetrucks would have to bounce to fires!

What if...
     the sidewalks from soft foam were made
          I could even fall off my bike and not need a
Band-aid!

What if...
     Aunt Sue went to give me a kiss
          I could jiggle and wiggle and she'd probably
miss!

                      (Oh, I'd like this!)

What if...
     my pizza, ice cream, and candy
          were made of soft foam—oh, how handy!

Whoops, hold on, and wait a minute!
     Foam cheese, toffee, and mint with chips in it
          it'd be light as a feather
          but taste like shoe leather

Forget the "What if's"—It's time to eat!
     I realize now real food can't be beat!

VERY SOFT BOWLING

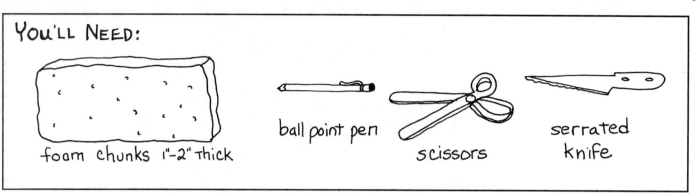

YOU'LL NEED:

foam chunks 1"-2" thick

ball point pen

scissors

serrated knife

WHAT TO DO:

1. Adult traces a large block letter onto foam with the ball point pen.

2. Adult uses large scissors to cut out letters. If necessary, use the serrated knife.

3. Set letters upright on sidewalk and roll ball at them. Variation: Make the whole alphabet. Have children name each as it falls.

Follow-up Activities

Letter Toss

Cut large letters out of a flat white bed sheet. (The cuts need to be large enough to toss one of your soft foam letters through.) Hang the sheet on a clothesline. Have children toss their foam letters through the same cut-out letter hole. For example, have them toss a Q through the Q hole. (Note: if a sheet and line are not available, have children toss the letter through a cardboard box with the letter cut out of it.)

Pop-up Letter

Shove or push a foam letter into a box that is just a bit smaller than the letter so that when a child opens it, the letter will "pop" (extend) out. Have children take turns secretly putting in different letters for the rest of their classmates to open.

Matching

Glue velcro strips to letters on signs or on a poster. Have children put the foam letter on top of the poster letter that it matches .

Letter Puzzles

• Cut letters out of a large piece of foam. Have children choose the letter that fits back into the right space.
• Cut a large foam letter into several pieces. Have children put the pieces back together to form the letter.

Letters Alive

Encourage children to interact with the large foam letters in a creative way. For example, have them think of all the things that they can do with the letter H--hug an H, hit an H, hurry home with an H, handshake with an H.

Sponge Printing

Cut out letters from new household sponges with scissors. Have children dip the letters into tempera paint that has been placed in styrofoam trays. Have them print on paper or cloth.

Wooly Stabiles

WATCH OUT FOR WINSTON

Winston was a cute, fuzzy, green caterpillar. He was extremely smart, but sometimes a little naughty. Winston ate everything in sight: leaves, flowers, fruit, and especially the vegetables in Mrs. Farnsworth's garden. Winston always knew that his habit of eating those vegetables would get him in trouble. This is the story of how he got caught.

Winston always found the tastiest tomatoes and cucumbers in Mrs. Farnsworth's garden. He would crawl along the soil, just under the leaves, and nibble as he went. Mrs. Farnsworth knew that something was eating her vegetables. And, one day , she complained out loud to her two grandchildren who were playing by the garden gate while she weeded around the broccoli.

"There is something eating by vegetables and when I find it, I'm going to squash it with my hoe!" she told the boy and girl who were busy bending pipe cleaners into alphabet letters.

Winston winced.

"I'd better find a good hiding place , " he said to himself.

First, he tried to curl around a carrot, but Mrs. Farnsworth thought she saw something move and began to dig around each one. Winston wiggled out just in time and found a spot under the cabbages. Then, Mrs. Farnsworth started picking up one cabbage at a time. Winston was worried. No place seemed safe.

Then, he spotted the two children playing by the gate. They were sitting on the ground bending fuzzy sticks to look like letters.

"What a perfect place to hide,"he said to himself. "Those fuzzy sticks look just like me-- only longer and straighter. I'll hide with them"

So Winston quietly crept over to the children and lay as straight as he could right next to a fuzzy stick.

Mrs. Farnsworth continued her search for the varmint, as she called it, while the children played.

"I've made a B and a K from these pipe cleaners. Do we have any more?" asked the little girl.

"Sure, there's a short, green fuzzy one over here," called the boy.

The little girl's hand reached over to Winston. He froze as she grabbed him. But he couldn't stay straight and wound around her fingers.

"Eek," she screamed as she tried to drop Winston. But the caterpillar just held on tighter.

Mrs. Farnsworth ran over to her granddaughter and grabbed Winston.

"So you are the varmint who's been eating my vegetables. Well, now I'm going to squash you. . ."

"No, Grandma," shouted both the boy and girl.

Mrs. Farnsworth stopped just as the hoe was about to come down on Winston's curled up fuzzy, green body.

"Could we have that caterpillar as a pet?' they asked. "We'll put him in a jar and feed him leaves and bits of vegetables. Then, we can see him spin a cocoon and later come out as a butterfly."

"You know," smiled Mrs. Farnsworth," That might be a good idea. We seem to have a very smart caterpillar here. He tried to pretend he was a pipe cleaner so I wouldn't catch him."

Winston couldn't believe it. He would not only be saved, but he would get to eat leaves and vegetables. As a "thank you," Winston curled up into a fuzzy W.

WOOLY STABILES

YOU'LL NEED:

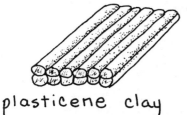

plasticene clay

large, craft-style pipe cleaners

WHAT TO DO:

1. Children roll, pat and mold plasticene clay into a ball. Flatten one side slightly by dropping ball on table.

2. Children twist pipe cleaners into letter shape. (Several pipe cleaner letters can be placed on clay base.)

3. Letter shapes are pushed into plasticene base.

Follow-up Activities

More Stabiles

Help children make letters from these other metal materials:
- Bell wire
- Floral wire
- Rolled or crushed-up aluminum foil

Letter Ring

Help children use any of the above, pliable, thin wires to shape a letter and make a loop the size of the ring finger. Secure with a twist at both ends.

"No- Fair-Looking" Letter

Have children bend and make letters with pipe cleaners with their hands under the table so they must feel how to shape the letter, rather than see it.

Large Straw Letters

Have children use pipe cleaners as joints to connect straws in order to shape letters. Add a touch of glue for permanence. Suspend them from the ceiling with string.

Bend and Guess

Start bending a wire into the shape of a letter. Whichever child first guesses which letter it is, as you are bending it, gets to whisper another letter in your ear.

ABC Caterpillar

Cut up egg cartons into individual cups. (You'll need 27 cups.) To make the head, draw a face onto one of the egg cups, and stick two pipe cleaner pieces in the top of the cup to resemble antennae. Holding the cup upside down , write one letter on each cup . Each time the class learns a new letter, attach another "letter cup" to your caterpillar with pipe cleaners poked through holes on the cup. Watch it grow!

X-tra Special Inks

☆ FIND THE LETTERS...

...IN THIS BUG   ...IN THIS BIRD

☆ HOW MANY LETTERS CAN YOU FIND?
TRACE EACH LETTER WITH YOUR FINGER.

HINTS:

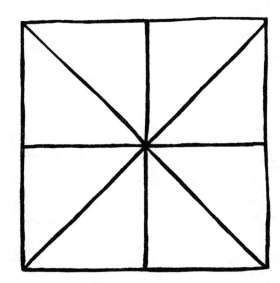

CAN YOU FIND:

T E M N F Z
X Y K

☆ HIDDEN LETTERS : FILL IN THE
MISSING PARTS

A HEBK7C

X-TRA SPECIAL INKS

INVISIBLE INK

YOU'LL NEED:

lemon juice
OR
white vinegar

Q-tips
or
Small brush

Porous paper
(newsprint)

iron
(adult use only)

WHAT TO DO:

1. Child dips Q-tip or brush into lemon juice or vinegar.

2. Child writes letters on paper with moistened Q-tip or brush.

3. Allow paper to dry thoroughly. (It will appear to be a blank paper.)

4. Adult heats iron to WARM and irons over entire paper. Letters will appear as paper is ironed.

BERRY INKS

YOU'LL NEED:

edible berries:
(collect or purchase)
  - Frozen blueberries
  - sliced stawberries
  - mulberries

non-breakable bowl
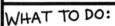

wooden spoon
stick pens with points
or
Quill feather pens
baby food jars
1 tsp. vinegar

WHAT TO DO:

1. Child places berries into bowl.

2. Child uses wooden spoon to crush berries until colorful juices are released.

3. Child dips pen or quills into ink and writes letters on sturdy paper.

4. If ink is not used immediately, store, tightly closed, in a baby food jar with one tsp. vinegar. Place in refrigerator.

Follow-up Activities

Instant Letter Surprise

Paint a white letter with tempera or poster paint onto white construction paper. Let it dry thoroughly. Brush India Ink over the whole paper covering the letter well. Let it dry. Have a child hold the black paper under running water and watch a white letter appear, as if by magic.

Natural Materials to Use with Ink

Take a nature hike and have children bring back materials to write with--feathers, phragmites, grass, twigs, cattails, foxtails. Encourage them to experiment with using a variety of natural materials and let them decide which ones work the best.

Batik Letters

Melt parafin wax in a double boiler or a one-pound coffee can set into a two-pound coffee can (Never melt wax over direct heat!) until liquid, but not too hot. Set container of melted wax into a container of very warm water and demonstrate how a brush can be used to spread liquid wax. Have children brush melted wax in the shape of letters onto a piece of 100% cotton fabric. Let dry thoroughly. Dip fabric into dyes or berry inks. Let dry. Iron off the wax placing layers of brown paper over the fabric.

Tracking

Using newspaper, have children go from left to right along the lines and from top to bottom to find and circle letters from "A" to "Z." Have them start at upper left of column and track with eyes and pencil until an "a" appears. Have them circle that "a" and continue tracking until a "b" appears, circle it, and continue until they find the whole alphabet.

Character Letters

Give each child a sheet of paper with a big India Ink letter drawn on it. Instruct everyone to make a weird funny creature out of the letter. Name creatures and share with the class.

Typewriter Letters

Obtain a typewriter and set it up with paper and other office equipment supplies so the children can "type a letter " when they play.

Letter Wheel

Cut out two seven-inch circles of posterboard. Cut a two-inch window out of one side of one circle. Put the two circles together with the window circle on top. Attach through the middle with a brass fastener. Move the top circle around and write one letter in the window onto the bottom circle. Move the bottom circle slightly clockwise and write another letter in the window. Make letters all around the circle so that when a child turns the window, she will see a different letter each time.

Yarn Letters

THE SAMPLER: A STORY OF LONG AGO

Hannah had a problem. She and her sisters went to the Goody Brown School for Young Girls. There, they learned to read and write letters and words and work with numbers. But Hannah could not learn all of her letters. When she picked up her slate and chalk, she just couldn't remember how to make one of the letters.

"*Well*," thought Hannah, "*I can make an I and an L and an O and an R, but I get all mixed up trying to make the Y.*"

Hannah was upset and worried.

One afternoon, her mother asked why she looked so unhappy.

"*Mama*," said Hannah. "*I can't learn all my letters. What can I do?*"

Mama thought for a few minutes, then said, " *I had that same trouble when I was your age. Your grandma taught me in a special way and I know it will work for you, too.*"

So Mama took out some cloth and pieces of yarn and a needle.

"*We will make a sampler using all the letters of alphabet!*" she exclaimed.

She showed Hannah how to make each letter by sewing them onto the cloth. Hannah made the Y even bigger than the rest of the letters. Hannah loved making the sampler. She learned to write all her letters very well, especially the Y. She even made a special "Thank You" sampler and gave it to her mother.

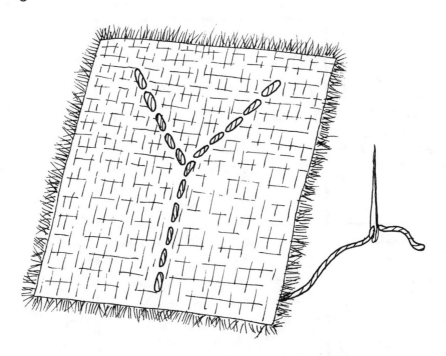

Yarn Letters

You'll Need:

 burlap (any color)

 chalk

 yarn

yarn needle

sewing machine (optional)

toothpick

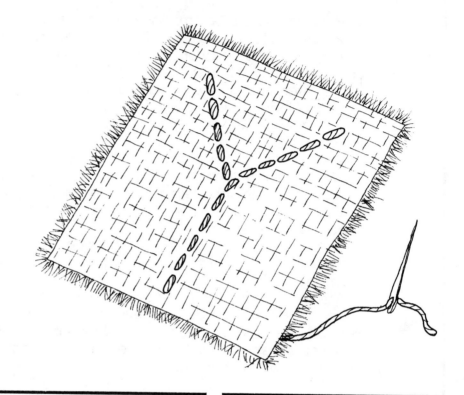

What To Do:

 1. Adult cuts a piece of burlap 10" x 10" for each letter sampler. Use a sewing machine to stay stitch 3/4" in from edges, if desired.

 2. Child fringes edges by pulling a few threads on each side. Use the toothpick to help, if necessary

 3. With chalk, adult or child draws a large outline of a letter centered on the burlap.

 4. Adult cuts an 18" length of yarn. Thread yarn through needle and knot one end.

 5. Child stitches letter using a medium-long stitch and goes from back to front to back again. Knot at finishing point.

 6. Variation: Older children might enjoy making a sampler with all the letters of the alphabet on it.

Follow-up Activities

Rope, Yarn, or String Letters

Help children spread glue on a piece of paper in the shape of a letter. Have them lay rope yarn or string over glue. Cut material at end of letter and let dry.

Yarn Hunt Game

Hide 8-inch to 12-inch pieces of yarn around the room. Instruct children to hunt for the yarn until they have enough to trace a giant stick letter that has been drawn on the floor. Let each child put the pieces of yarn that he finds on the letter.

String-a-letter

Hammer nails into a piece of scrap wood in the shape of a letter. Knot one end of a long piece of yarn onto one nail. Have children wind string around the nails one at a time (like dot-to-dot) to connect the nails into a letter shape.

Letter Mobile

Attach colorful paper letters to pieces of string. Tape the strings to each end of plastic straws. Make as many as desired. Tie a string to the middle of one of these straws and suspend. Keep taping more letter straws, with more strings added in the middle, to previously suspended straws so that you have a long, hanging mobile. Suspend from the ceiling and watch the letters move in a natural or child-blown breeze. Challenge children to make just one of the letters move.
• *Variation* Instead of using all letters on the mobile, choose one letter and pictures of things that begin with that letter.

Follow the String (or Yarn) Game

Tie a letter to one end of a small ball of string (or yarn). Hide the letter. Do not tell children what the letter is. Unroll the ball of string or yarn in maze fashion around the room until it is completely unwound and hand one child the free end. Have the child follow the yarn until he reaches the letter. This is more fun if you have three or four children doing this at the same time. For use as a party game, the letter can correspond with a gift or favor that is found at the end of the string.

Letter Laundry

String a line across the room. Have children attach paper, cardboard, or fabric letters with clothespins. You can also put a letter on the line along with an object or picture of an object that begins with that letter.

Cross Stitch on Gingham

Mark (with a light pencil) a large letter on a piece of gingham using X's in each tiny square. Have older children stitch with needle and embroidery thread over the X's to make the letter.

Zoo Box

Z

A ZOO ALPHABET

*(Read these rhyming couplets to children.
They will enjoy illustrating
them and saying then over and over. Use
these rhymes to make up more of your own
with other animals..)*

A   An alligator's creepy crawl
   Frightens and scares one and all.

B   Up high in a tree a bird safely sat
   Whistling a challenge to a prowling cat.

C   Quickly but quietly a cat crept around
   Hunting and hoping for a mouse to be
found.

D   A duck swims circles on the pond
   And eats all the fish of which he is fond.

E   The gray elephand waits quietly and paces
   For peanuts from children with smiling faces.

F   The little green frog who lives in a bog
   Comes out at noon to sun on a log.

G   The giraffe eats leaves from a tall tree;
   His luncheon meal is always free.

H   The horse is an animal commonly seen;
   It can plow fields or even carry a queen.

I   The iguana is a tropical lizard
   Who never fears getting caught in a blizzard.

J   The jaguar is a really fast cat;
   He leaps and jumps and does things like that.

K   The mother kangaroo loves to hop;
   Her baby does too and never wants to stop.

L   The lion is a creature wild;
   Yet, quiet and mindful until he's riled.

M   A moose is loose, but don't you fear;
   He's just a cousin of the gentle deer.

N   A bird in a nest perched under a roof
   Looks down on us and remains aloof

O   The octopus has tentacles eight
   But he still can't open the garden gate.

P   The penguin waddles to and fro,
   Loves the cold, and is always dressed just so.

Q   The quail is a quiet little bird
   Who can walk in fields; and not be heard.

R   The rabbit is a quiet chap;
   Yet, when in danger, his foot will tap.

S   The menacing snake wiggles side to side;
   Yet, when we meet, he's the first to hide.

T   The turtle walks so very slow;
   Perhaps he just has no place to go.

U   The unicorn is a mythical creature
   Whose golden horn is his best feature.

V   The vulture sits around and frowns;
   He has some ups, but many more downs.

W   The whale is a mighty ocean beast
   Who considers tiny shrimp a perfect feast.

X   Xtra special is each animal in the zoo;
   They all are treasures for me and you.

Y   The yak is an ox with long, silky hair;
   Cold Tibet is his home and he needs it there.

Z   The zebra looks like one of the horse types;
   But his body is white with black patterned
stripes.

ZOO BOX

YOU'LL NEED:

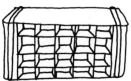

one 24 section
wood soda box

26 wooden
alphabet blocks

plastic, rubber, cardboard
or clay or playdough
molded animals - one
for each letter of alphabet

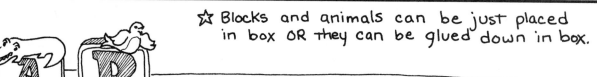

☆ Blocks and animals can be just placed
in box OR they can be glued down in box.

☆ Children can arrange blocks in A-B-C order from left to right.

☆ Children can match animals with letter blocks in box.

☆ Children can hunt for other objects to place in box with blocks.

Follow-up Activities

Wooden Letters

Make wooden letters out of:
- Green or fresh twigs and sticks (Tie together with dental floss.)
- Toothpicks or ice cream sticks (Lay them on paper and glue.)
- Scrap wood cubes (Paint a letter on each side.)
- Block letters (Use unit blocks to make a giant letter on the floor in which the children can sit.)

Thumb Tack Letters

Help children knock thumbtacks into a block of soft wood, such as pine, in the shape of a letter.

Pegboard Letters

Chalk a letter shape onto a pegboard. Have children trace the outline of the letter by inserting pegs into the board.

Earth Letters

Use wooden sticks that children have found on a nature walk to draw letters in the mud or sand.

Stick Letters

Tape or staple cardboard letters onto ice cream sticks or dowels.
Use these letters:
- In an alphabet parade
- As stick puppets in an alphabet play
- In an alphabet hunt. Insert sticks randomly throughout the yard. Have children hunt for the sticks, pick them up, bring them to you, and identify them. When they really know the alphabet, have them pick the letters up in ABC order.
- In a treasure hunt. Insert sticks into the ground so that the children can follow them from point A to point B and so on, without skipping, until they reach point Z where a treasure (such as a balloon, tiny toy, or bag of popcorn) can be found.

ABC Pick-Up Sticks

Write one letter of the alphabet on each end of 26 ice cream sticks. Have one child at a time play by dropping the 26 sticks on the floor. He has to pick up one at a time without moving any of the others. As long as he does this, he continues playing and keeps all the sticks. When he moves one other stick, he loses his turn and the next child takes his place.

Have an Alphabet Party

Celebrate the learning of all the letters with a festive Alphabet Party. Have parents join you to commemorate this important accomplishment in the lives of their children.

Parties are wonderful not only for the festivities themselves, but their planning and preparation make great learning experiences for children. Include them in all phases of pre-party preparation. Children can help make reproduced invitation pages pretty with the addition of drawn, stamped, or pasted-on letters. They can not only plan the food, but make some of it. Learning songs beforehand will help children sing out confidently and act as models for their parents. Games can be learned ahead of time to lessen confusion during the party.

The following are some suggestions for your Alphabet Party. Choose the ones that would interest and be appropriate for your children and parents.

Invitations

Type or write out the necessary information and reproduce for each child. Your invitation might read:

"You are invited to join our class for a potluck Alphabet Party. Your letter is _____. (Fill in one different letter for each family.) Please bring in something to eat that begins with this letter or is in the shape of this letter (cookies, a cake, pretzels, for example) We will be sharing food and fun, so please join us. R.S.V.P."

Use any of the techniques suggested throughout this book to decorate the invitations. They might look nice stamped, , collaged, with yarn glued on, or with letter rubbings.

Decorations

- Display the decorative letters that you've made during the year: (the banner, paper mache letters, sculptured letters.)
- Hang letter chains on walls and ceiling.
- Display an alphabet photo mural. (See page 68.)
- Use large foam letters to spell out WELCOME. (See page 100.)
- Help children make placemats of paper with their names written in large letters. Or, roll out long strips of paper down long tables and have children decorate "their places."

Food

Although most of the food will be brought in by parents, children will enjoy a cooperative cooking project for the party. Use tiny alphabet pasta to make a soup (See page 77 for the recipe.) or make a cold salad with cut-up vegetables and salad dressing. Combine apple juice, a bottle of lemon-flavored soda, and cranberry juice to make ABC Punch.

Dress

The Alphabet Party is the perfect time for children to wear their "I Know the Alphabet" T-shirts. (See page 17.) Parents might be encouraged to wear any of the many t-shirts with sayings that are available.

Instead of nametags, parents and children can wear initial tags. This makes a great ice breaker as parents try to guess other guests' names by just seeing the initial.

Entertainment

• *A Song* What would start off a fun party like this better than children, dressed in their special T-shirts, standing and singing the "Alphabet Song" one time around and having parents join in?
• *Drama* Children might enjoy acting out one of the poems or the play (See page 47.) in this book as you narrate it.

Games

Spend the rest of the time playing games both children and parents can enjoy. Games found throughout this book can be fun if you've found ones that are particular favorites of the children (bean bag scatter, hunt letters on a stick, musical letters and so on).

• *"I'd Like to Get to Know You"* When everyone has an initial nametag, ask them all to group themselves according to their first initial. Everyone will have fun seeing who else has a name that begins with their letter. Kim will love to know that there are Keiths, Karens, Kates, Kerrys, and Kens that share her initial. Ask each group to *"Give me a K (or L and so on)."* "Have them respond by shouting out their group's initial. This is a rousing way to either start or end a great party
• *Letter Telephone* Have everyone sit in a circle. (Make two circles if there are too many people). Have one child start by picking a small letter out of a box and looking at it without letting anyone else see it. Have him hold it in a closed fist. Have him whisper the letter to the person sitting next to him and pass on the letter and have that person whisper the letter to the next person and pass it on, and so on. No one is allowed to look at the letter until the message gets to the last person in the circle who announces what was whispered and looks in his hand to see if it is right.
• *Pin the Letter on the Alphabet* Draw the letters of the alphabet sequentially left to right along a long, large strip (or taped pieces) of paper. Attach the mural to a wall about four feet high.

Have each person take a turn holding one cut-out paper letter of the alphabet and try to "pin it on" the correct place on this long alphabet mural. You might want to blindfold the person and give a twist or two. However, point them in the approximate direction that they can go to match letters.

After everyone has taken a turn, see which person has come

closest to pinning his letter onto the correct position of that letter in the alphabet. Those people who come closest are the winners.

Party Favors

Some of the crafts suggested in this book can be made beforehand and taken home as party favors. You might consider using bendable beads, chocolate or cookie letters, puffy cottton, dough letter decorations, stenciled family flags (Stencil family members' initials onto a piece of flag-shaped fabric and wrap it around a dowel.)
• *Children's Alphabet Book* Each time a paper-type craft is made, have children put it in their special alphabet folder. Have them decorate the cover of the folder with cut-out letters. At the end of the year, before the party, assemble the papers by stapling them into book form. Give one to each child to take home as a memory of learning their letters and of the fun projects on which they have worked.

A B C D

E F G H I

J K L M N

O P Q R

S T U V

W X Y Z

CRAYONS CRAFTS AND CONCEPTS

by

Kathy Faggella

Art activities can teach basic concepts and be integrated into the whole curriculum. Presented in one page, easy-to-read formats, that even your children can follow, these 50+ projects will fit into each theme and subject area, you introduce. There are also suggestions for setting up an art area, making smocks, safety rules, and follow ups for each activity. Projects are designed to be reproduced and sent home for follow up, too.

TABLE OF CONTENTS

- All about Me
- The Seasons
- Colors
- Shapes
- Language Development
- Children's Literature
- Celebrations and Holidays
- Science
- Opposites
- Math
- Feelings

TO ORDER:

Send $9.95 (plus $1 for each book's postage and handling) to:

First Teacher, Inc.
Box 29
60 Main St.
Bridgeport, CT. 06602

OR CALL: 1-800-341-1522

NEW BOOKS from FIRST TEACHER

Partners for Learning is based on the be-lief that parents and teachers are part-ners in the education of young children. The book is a guide to the development of positive parent participation in schools—from orientation meetings and potluck parent/child meals to parent-sponsored fundraisers and parent vol-unteer projects. It's a must for the caring classroom!

Unique in its organized approach to the teaching of thinking skills to young chil-dren, this book offers a great variety of activities for each area of the classroom and curriculum. Each activity develops a specific thinking skill. In addition, there are suggestions for developing creativity and problem-solving skills.

An anthology of the best ideas for cele-brations from FIRST TEACHER, this book is based on the experience of hundreds of early childhood teachers. From origi-nal ideas for traditional holidays and seasonal celebrations to birthday parties in school and multi-cultural special events, this book will show you how to teach your children that every day is worth celebrating.

A comprehensive guide to integrating children's literature into all areas of the early childhood curriculum. There are hundreds of annotated book sugges-tions, each with a motivating or follow-up activity.

TO ORDER:

Send $9.95 (plus $1 for each book's postage and handling) to:

First Teacher, Inc.
Box 29
60 Main St.
Bridgeport, CT 06602

OR CALL:
1-800-341-1522

From the authors of
CRAYONS CRAFTS AND CONCEPTS

CONCEPT COOKERY

by
Kathy Faggella

Through cooking experiences in the preschool classroom, children can develop basic skills and concepts. Organized by themes and concept areas, these 50+child and classroom tested recipes will fit naturally into your curriculum.

Easy-to-read, sequential recipe charts will appeal to your children as much as they do to you. Single page formats can easily be copied and sent home for parent follow up.

TABLE OF CONTENTS
- All about Me
- The Seasons
- Colors
- Shapes
- Science
- Opposites
- Math
- Language Development
- Children's Literature
- Celebrations and Holidays

Q: WHERE CAN YOU FIND HUNDREDS OF CLASSROOM TESTED IDEAS *EACH MONTH* TO HELP YOUR CHILDREN LEARN AND GROW?

A: IN FIRST TEACHER

Each 16 page issue of FIRST TEACHER provides you with innovative projects to make each day an exciting new adventure. We give you ideas for toymaking, games and recipes to do with young children. We take you to the world of make believe with ideas for drama and creative movement. And experts recommend the very best books for young children in FIRST TEACHER.

FIRST TEACHER has a newspaper format, but it's something to read and save. Each issue has a topical theme, so each one adds a permanent resource of projects and ideas to your school or center.

FIRST TEACHER is written by experienced caregivers, daycare directors, and nursery teachers, so it's full of tested ideas to help you guide and motivate young children

FIRST TEACHER has been read and used by over 30,000 Early Childhood teachers. Here's what one of them, Racelle Mednikow, preschool teacher for 16 years, says:

"What a pleasure to be provided with well written, resourceful and usable ideas that can be interjected into our everyday curriculum and be of true value to each of our teachers!"

"Thank you so much for this delightful, informative newspaper."

Subscribe today! Don't miss another month of ideas, projects, and activities.

SUBSCRIBE
TODAY
AT
THIS SPECIAL
INTRODUCTORY
PRICE! **$17.95**
($6.05 OFF THE REGULAR PRICE)

Write to: FIRST TEACHER
Box 29
60 Main Street
Bridgeport, CT 06602

Or call: 1-800-341-1522
(8AM - 9PM Mon. - Fri.
9AM - 5PM Sat.)